MEMBER OF PARLIAMENT

Member of Parliament

JOHN GRANT, MP

LONDON
MICHAEL JOSEPH

First published in Great Britain by Michael Joseph Ltd
52 Bedford Square, London WC1B 3EF
1974

ISBN 0 7181 1218 0

Set and printed in Great Britain by
Tonbridge Printers Ltd, Peach Hall Works, Tonbridge, Kent
in Times ten on twelve point on paper supplied by
P. F. Bingham Ltd, and bound by Dorstel Press
Harlow

Contents

Introduction

There is no average Member of Parliament, no single MP who typifies his Westminster colleagues. MPs are as diverse a bunch of individuals as it is possible to find under any one roof.

All that I claim for this book is that it gives a fair personal portrayal of the working life of one MP over a Parliamentary year and that, in doing so, it should assist materially towards a better understanding of just how the people ordinary folk elect to represent them go about their business.

I reject the verdict of those cynics who contend that few people care about what their Parliamentary representatives are up to. And I suggest that Parliamentary democracy, whatever its short-comings, retains the overwhelming allegiance of the British people. Yet there is a detectable resentment among an increasingly aware and articulate population, that Parliament seems remote and unable to reflect adequately their hopes and aspirations.

There is something of a vacuum to be filled. When an opinion poll shows that although 71 per cent of people are interested, either fairly or very much, in what goes on in Parliament yet 77 per cent admit they know nothing or 'not very much' about the place, the grounds for disquiet are as great as the room for mis-conception about the work of MPs.

There is an unsatisfied demand for far more knowledge about Westminster and every reason to seek to meet it. This quest for knowledge is highlighted in the question I have so often been asked during my own short Parliamentary life: 'What's it like, being a MP?'

That is the question I have really set out to answer by building up a picture of my own operations both in Parliament and in my under-privileged constituency, though not by seeking to establish any kind of all-embracing record of my activity in either place.

7

This is an insider's story of an institution which is often absurd, irritating and archaic, but nonetheless fascinating and important to our way of life. The Palace of Westminster is a rambling, sprawling, bewildering place to the visitor or newcomer. Spend a year or two there as a MP and you recognise what a small community you live in.

I have had no truck with tearoom tittle-tattle or dinner table gossip of the kind that can add nothing worthwhile to the public appreciation of how Parliament ticks. But I have made no such reservations concerning policies and the issues of the day, together with the personalities involved in them and have commented candidly on these though I happily plead guilty to Party prejudice.

I have tried to reveal much of Parliament's inner workings and to show the tedium and turbulence alike. Who are the 'big' men in debate who can fill the Chamber? What are working conditions like for Members? Is the Heath-Wilson feud as bitter across the Despatch Box as the Press Gallery reporters make it sound?

How much notice do MPs take of their postbags? I describe how they work locally as ombudsmen-cum-welfare officers, trying to resolve a multiplicity of differing problems, usually with inadequate facilities and with prestige rather than authority as the most potent weapon with which to combat bureaucracy on behalf of frustrated constituents.

This book was suggested to me as a Backbencher by literary agent Giles Gordon whose subsequent comments helped greatly as it progressed. He sought a MP-journalist, sufficiently fresh to the Commons to be able to write frankly, without the chip on the shoulder which often accompanies unfulfilled ambition and without the overfamiliarity with the subject which leads to the assumption that any layman understands 'that' – so why bother to explain it. Since then I have been given a Front Bench role. That has made no difference in my approach to the story.

Politicians fared badly in 1973. Scandals involving them were worldwide, headed by the United States Watergate fiasco. Names like Poulson and Lonhro, plus the Lambton-Jellicoe call-girl affair, all added discredit at home.

Despite the warts most MPs deserve more support for their efforts than they receive and more, not less, power to be able to improve their limited effectiveness as watchdogs over Government.

This book will, I hope, underline these points. Above all, I trust it will contribute towards breaching the undoubted communications gap that exists between the pollticians and the public whose interests they represent.

John Grant, MP

October

1st, Sunday: Inevitably, the pundits pedal up and down the columns of their newspapers on the eve of the Labour Party's annual conference, speculating endlessly about the extent of the disaster about to befall us as a Party. What they say is usually swiftly forgotten. As an ex-reporter I well know the truth of that old Fleet-street quip about today's paper: 'It's all fish and chips tomorrow'.

It's just as well that memories are short. By the end of conference week everything usually seems a lot less dramatic and significant.

Will this year's conference prove extraordinarily different? Will there be a major crisis over the bid to commit us to all out opposition in principle to Common Market membership and how will Harold Wilson play it? What effect will Prime Minister Heath's proposed package deal on pay and prices have on the delegates? Will the unions play into his hands by demanding total rejection without offering their counter-proposals?

These were the main questions which I pondered on the tedious motorway drive to Blackpool, the conference venue I dislike most. I sometimes think the Labour Party suffers from an inverted snobbery about Blackpool and pretends it likes the place. I rate it garish, scruffy and over-crowded. There's no grass along the seafront but some of the concrete is painted green. It's their gesture towards the quality of life.

This evening I went to a cocktail party given by the Transport and General Workers' Union and attended by Harold Wilson and most of the Party and trade union leaders. I heard that the Party Executive had a fair old rumpus in its private meeting during the afternoon about the way to handle the Common Market issue at

11

the conference. The engineering workers' motion seeking a straight 'No' to the Market on principle will be opposed by the platform. But the executive voted by 13–12 to support a boilermakers' union motion calling for renegotiation on terms which are sure to be impossible to obtain. Even so, the vital thing for Harold Wilson, who is to make the keynote speech on the issue, is that a National Executive Committee statement will also be put to the conference. That carries much less restrictive terms and he can support that without embarrassment. But it's a bit of a tightrope he has to tread.

2nd Monday: It's a long time since a Labour Party leader has been so vilified by the media as Tony Wedgwood Benn has been in the treatment meted out to him recently. I don't share all his views and I think his timing is often atrocious. But much of the hostility can be quite easily explained. It is the natural reaction of an establishment which finds itself under open challenge. There is no organised conspiracy against him in my opinion. There doesn't need to be.

He has taken full advantage of his year as Labour Party chairman – a job filled by 'Buggins turn' from the Executive members according to their seniority of service. He is under fire from a lot of people in the Party who feel he is making a bid to establish himself in any possible leadership contest. Unless Harold gets into real trouble over the Market this week no such situation arises, or will arise for a very long time. Tony is suffering from over-exposure at the moment but he doesn't appear to recognise it.

Still, his chairman's speech was decidely low-key. That may be a good sign. At the recent TUC conference in Brighton his fraternal address on behalf of the Party went down very well indeed. But he's been a good deal less restrained since.

These annual conferences are always a hubbub of fringe meetings, cocktail parties and dinners once the day's conference proceedings are over. Sometimes the fringe meetings can be more interesting then the conference. Speakers are sometimes more candid away from the inhibiting influence of the TV cameras. I visited several functions tonight, including the first birthday party for 'Labour Weekly', the Party's official newspaper for which I write a fortnightly comment column. Harold and Mary Wilson turned up. Harold was asked to cut the cake. He grinned at Tony Wedgwood Benn and said: 'Tony has been telling me to stick the knife in all week.'

3rd Tuesday: The conference only really got off the ground today. It did so with Harold Wilson's speech on the Parliamentary Report, ostensibly a summary of what Labour MPs have been doing during the past year. Harold spent most of his time savaging Heath and the Tories. There was no shortage of ammunition. It was one of those clever tactical exercises which he carried out so well. For a man whose back is allegedly against the wall, it was a confident effort and earned him the usual standing ovation. I can't say I care much for this sort of gesture unless it's truly spontaneous. But it's become a ritual and it looks like a snub if you don't join in. Thank heaven we don't do it like the Tories. Their adulation is reminiscent of a Nuremberg rally.

Poplar's MP Ian Mikardo made a powerful speech on behalf of the Executive, calling for a large and rapid extension of the public sector. That was easy. Everyone's a Clause Four man now.

'Mik', as Left-wing as they come, was last year's Party chairman. He was quite a contrast to Tony Benn. Benn has leaned over backwards to give rank-and-file delegates their rights and has seemed almost to invite frustrating technical points of order. His yen for participation has got a bit out of control, however worthy the intentions. 'Mik' ran the conference with a guile that was as professional as it was unscrupulous. You pays your money and takes your choice. There is no doubt that the conference veterans, in particular the old union 'pros', are highly critical of Benn. But he's going down pretty well with ordinary delegates.

This evening at the Fire Brigades Union party I discussed the pay situation with two of the men who are most likely to be there when the crunch comes. They were Alan Fisher, the voluble general secretary of the National Union of Public Employees, and Jack Biggin, the General and Municipal Workers' Union man who is the union side secretary in the electricity supply industry negotiating body. Fisher, just elected to the TUC's

Economic Committee, knows the limits of his industrial strength. A dustman's strike is unpleasant but the effects are not immediate. Nonetheless, his union, along with others, want £4 a week more for the local government workers.

The power station men want more than that. They really do have the industrial muscle. The Government knows it. Biggin believes that Heath, by apparently singling out the public sector to kick off its £2 pay policy limit, is just fueling the militants. This is one group of workers the Government can't beat, not even with statutory backing. All the more reason for staying away from legal sanctions until this particular claim is out of the way, even if the price is high. Either Heath will see the sense of that argument or he will become involved in a confrontation which he can't win. Could this claim provoke a General Election? It's a question that's being asked but I think any conflict over it will be too soon for that. Heath wants us as inextricably as possible in the Common Market before he risks his Government at the polls.

4th, Wednesday: We got a spontaneous standing ovation today. It went to Michael Foot and was quite something. Five minutes at the rostrum for his Common Market contribution wasn't long enough to let him really get his dander up. But Michael has become a sort of Laurence Olivier of the political scene, almost to be revered. Since his acceptance of Front Bench responsibilities in Parliament and his election to the Shadow Cabinet, his support is no longer confined to the Left-wing. Next year he will be on the platform at conference after his runaway victory in the elections for the Party Executive.

Harold Wilson scored again in the Market debate with another skilful tactical delivery. Then came the card votes – the system which gives the unions dominance of conference because of their giant block votes, related to their affiliated membership. And Harold got what he wanted. There was a handsome majority for the National Executive Committee statement on renegotiation, a much smaller majority for the boilermakers' motion and a defeat, albeit narrow, for the uncompromising anti-Market engineering workers' motion.

It was not surprising that Harold was in jaunty form at the

Co-op's social gathering when he arrived shortly before midnight. He wisecracked that he may have got there late but 'I'm not the late Leader as some people have been forecasting.'

5th, Thursday: The big economic debate was overshadowed by Heath's £2 package.

My good friend Percy Coldrick, the general secretary of the Transport Salaried Staffs Association, the rail clerks' union, moved a motion which was carried on a card vote. It means the Party is again formally in favour of a prices and incomes policy. What kind of a policy that will be is another matter. But it will be interesting to see in the months ahead if those members of the Parliamentary Labour Party who have tended to argue that conference decisions are sacrosanct, will work to arrive at an acceptable formula on this which will help to get another Labour Government elected. Some hope.

Ray Buckton, another old friend, is in a very different position from Percy. He represents the locomen, the craftsmen on the railways. He wants absolutely no truck at all with Heath's £2 ceiling for pay rises nor with any narrowing of pay differentials. He made this clear from the rostrum and it left me concerned at the position under a Labour Government which would be faced with the same problem. If Heath gets no help what about us? So much, though, will depend on the rest of the economic and social package we devise.

Denis Healey made the main platform speech. He had a difficult task. So much had already been covered earlier in the week, mainly by Harold Wilson. But although his was an unexciting performance, it was solid enough. He has rapidly grasped his new portfolio as Shadow Chancellor and if there is any question of a change in the leadership in, say, the next three to five years, I doubt if Healey will be far away.

I hoped to speak on pensions in this afternoon's debate on the social services but so did around 70 other delegates and I wasn't called. I intended to urge that the next Labour Government really does give this priority and to refer to a case I dealt with just before leaving for Blackpool concerning an 80-year-old disabled pensioner in my constituency who faced having her phone cut off because she couldn't pay the bill. Still, it's a speech I shan't waste. I have a lot to do with the pensioners in my constituency and I'll use it there.

I left for home just before the conference ended for the day. I knew there would be a pile of correspondence to catch up on and I had my Friday night constituency advice bureau, usually referred to as 'the surgery', to attend.

6th, Friday: Tony Wedgwood Benn has done it again. His closing remarks to the conference which I watched on television have given a disproportionate boost to the coverage by the media of the resignation of Lincoln's pro-Market Labour MP, Dick Taverne. It's all great stuff for the newspapers and TV to get hold of and project.

As always, there is a lot in what Tony Benn has to say. He presumably feels that attack is the best form of defence. That approach is often mistaken. Now the Press will keep the story in the headlines for days with charge and counter-charge and Taverne will receive a thoroughly undue amount of free publicity. Tony could have made his criticisms of the media but left Taverne right out of the reckoning.

Tonight I went, as usual, to the 'surgery'. It's almost impossible to assess in advance how long one of these stints will last. I hold them at our Party rooms, just off Highbury Corner. I try to start punctually at 7 o'clock because a session can easily last for 2 to $2\frac{1}{2}$ hours, although $1\frac{1}{2}$ hours is about normal.

Sometimes a few cases take quite a time to handle. Sometimes you can whistle through a lot, speedily and effectively. Quite a few people come as much to get something off their chests as for help. They need someone to talk to and, though it isn't the most productive use of your time, oddly enough you can aid them on occasion just by listening. Obviously that's not what you are really there for and you hope to be able to get positive results whenever there is justification for action. You are always conscious of the clock, of the other people still downstairs in the waiting room, of the Party workers in the next room who want a word with you as soon as you are free, maybe of your desire to have a beer and some rather more relaxing chat, and of the simple fact that you have a home to get back to.

One thing I can be sure of in advance: that most of the cases will involve housing problems. We have a housing waiting list of well over 10,000 in Islington. They come in desperation, sometimes in tears, over their slum conditions. Some people have been on the waiting list for years. I always explain carefully that I have no powers in housing locally but that I will ensure that the Council know about the problem and will pass on the reply. It's very wrong to raise false hopes and I know that my success rate in these cases is low. It has to be. People think their MP has some magic wand to wave. That couldn't be justified. It would imply queue-jumping, as often as not. On the other hand, some cases don't seem to get adequate attention and you can at least remedy that with a worthwhile result here and there.

You get them all in Islington. It's that kind of place. They bring you their tax and social security problems, their legal problems, their marital difficulties, their consumer complaints. They want action against the police on behalf of a jailed husband or son, over their blocked drains and their children's education. You name it, I've known it. Often it's a matter of getting them in contact with the relevant authority to look into their case.

There's tragedy and comedy. Sometimes they overlap. It can be hard to know whether to laugh or cry.

It can be extraordinarily offbeat. Quite recently a young actress turned up to tell me she intended to set fire to herself outside a West End theatre company's offices in protest against their alleged treatment of her. Apparently, she had been sacked from a part. She appeared to be in earnest and disinclined to accept my advice to abandon her plan. She quoted George Bernard Shaw to me as, in effect, stating that if a protest is worth doing it's worth doing well. I pointed out to her that Shaw never set fire to himself in his life of campaigning and lived to a ripe old age.

It was all very mundane stuff tonight, however. Only a handful of people, with the inevitable emphasis on housing. I was away in about 1½ hours.

8th, Sunday: The *Sunday People* newspaper today carried a story by its political editor Terry Lancaster which involves me. Lancaster is an ex-Fleet Street colleague of mine and I had discussed the details with him in Blackpool last week.

It arose from my link with the Civil and Public Services

Association, the biggest of the Civil Service trades unions, for which I act as Parliamentary consultant. That means I keep an eye on things happening in the Common which might affect their members and the union, in turn, keeps me posted about developments in its field which have Parliamentary implications. It gives me a very useful special interest inside the Commons and also enables me to keep more closely in touch with the trades unions than might otherwise be the case. For instance, I was invited by the union to attend the TUC conference at Brighton in September, along with its delegation, and was thus one of the few Labour MPs to be there for the week.

The union's general secretary, Bill Kendall, was very disturbed to learn about an appointment made by John Davies, the Secretary of State for Trade and Industry. It was this situation which I talked to Lancaster about. Davies has appointed a Tory Central Office man, John Cope, as his Special Assistant to work inside his private office but to help with the political aspects of his work, particularly as it affects the Tory Party outside Parliament. I have tabled Parliamentary questions to both Heath and Davies to be answered when Parliament resumes.

It seems quite wrong to Bill Kendall, and to me, that this man should have this kind of access and terms of reference which go far beyond those enjoyed by the previous Labour Government's outsiders who were brought into Whitehall. The Tories will, of course, put up a smokescreen and allege that Labour did it too, but I don't think they can sustain that one. Bill has written to the National Whitley Council Staff Side, the union side of the Civil Service negotiating machinery, asking for enquiries to be made.

Lancaster wrote: 'There's a first-class row brewing...' He could be right. I shall certainly pursue the matter although the important thing is to get it aired quickly and I've done that.

9th Monday: I had a call this morning from the Headmistress of Highbury Hill High School for Girls asking me to confirm that I will be the guest speaker at the school prize-giving. I accepted in the knowledge that there is rather more in this engagement than meets the eye.

Education is a real 'hot potato' in Islington at the moment and Highbury Hill High is straight out of the oven. It's a grammar school. Dr Eric Briault, the Inner London Education Authority's Education Officer, has produced sweeping reorganisation proposals which would mean the school's demise.

I am utterly opposed to the retention of grammar schools and consider that while they exist the so-called 'sink' schools, the less desirable second class establishments to which many parents seek to avoid sending their kids, will never disappear. But Briault's closure scheme is not necessarily the answer. It has yet to be discussed by the ILEA, which is Labour controlled. But scores of parents have written to me. Some letters are angry, some anxious. Even my predecessor as East Islington's MP, now Lord Fletcher, has been in touch with me to express his concern as an ex-governor of the school.

None of this is my direct responsibility. It is one more example of constituents seeking to pin down the wrong man. Not that I blame them. It can have some effect. Indeed, I have written to Briault to underline the concern felt and have been in touch with the three elected ILEA members for the area. These are the people, of course, that the parents must chase and many have done so. I am relieved to hear that our trio of councillors have come up with a compromise plan. It should take some of the heat out of the controversy. No one can satisfy the 'hands off the grammar schools' brigade. They will only fade away when we get really good comprehensives throughout the borough by levelling up, rather than levelling down. The snag is that that means spending a lot of money. Noticeably, it is the same bunch of pro-grammar school Tories who consistently attack the ILEA for spending too much.

11th, Wednesday: My General Election opponent, Richard Devonald-Lewis, stole the early limelight when the Tory Party circus opened at Blackpool today. I saw the TV flashback which showed him nipping in to the rostrum to accuse his Party bosses of only picking out self-congratulatory motions for discussion and wanting to indulge in a white-washing exercise.

I once attended a Tory conference as a journalist and found it obscenely undemocratic. I have no doubt Devonald-Lewis was right. Above all, he secured himself excellent publicity which was doubtless the real purpose of his outburst.

Good luck to him in that. Politicians who pretend to despise publicity are usually those without the wit or gumption to acquire it. Devonald-Lewis works at it and does extremely well locally. I can't grumble. My mileage in the local Press is pretty vast and I take some pains over supplying my own 'news service'. Publicity, propaganda, call it what you will. If you aren't interested in getting your views across, you shouldn't be in politics.

Devonald-Lewis lost to me at the last General Election by more than 5,000 votes. Like me, he has been re-selected by his local Party to fight the new constituency of Islington Central at the next General Election. I don't rate Devonald-Lewis as the man to start a landslide. He is the local echo of Enoch Powell – 'a pocket Powell', I once dubbed him – and Powell is godfather to his baby son. Even the family cat is called Enoch. At 32, he's got time on his side if he is serious about looking for a seat that will get him into Parliament. It won't happen in Islington.

12th, Thursday: The local Trades Council had a meeting tonight in the Co-operative Hall in Seven Sisters Road, the boundary road between my constituency and North Islington. Subject: the Government's Housing Finance Act.

It became obvious that inducing Islington tenants to withhold their rents in protest against the Act was very much in the minds of some of the more militant people there.

Gerry Southgate, Leader of the Labour-controlled Islington Borough Council, spoke first. He explained lucidly enough what the Council's reluctant decision to implement the Tory Act would mean in terms of increases to tenants and how the Council hoped to make use of the rebate scheme. Gerry is able and articulate but when he finished no one raised a handclap. His line of moderation was not what most of the audience of fifty or so wanted to hear.

The next speaker was a tenants' federation man from outside the Borough. He launched a violent attack on the Tories but also castigated councils like Islington which have opted to operate the Act. He got plenty of applause.

I spoke next – for about ten minutes. I also hit out at the Government for turning council housing into a profit-making affair and for compelling councils to raise rents unnecessarily and inequitably just when Heath was appealing for wage restraint. I felt obliged to say though that although some modifications to the Act might yet be secured, it is here to stay until a Labour Government repeals it, as we are now pledged firmly to do. I could see that didn't go down too well with those who believe the Tories might yet be forced to at least 'put it on ice' as a result of tenant or even trades union action. I don't reckon these folk are being realistic. I ended with a direct assault on Heath for talking on the eve of the Tory conference about those who bully and shout. I said hundreds of local councils, including Islington's, would tell him: 'If you want to see a bully Mr Heath, look in the mirror.' The applause for all this was somewhat tepid. I suppose I should have been grateful to have got some.

George Cunningham, South-west Islington's Labour MP, followed on briefly and then there was general discussion from the floor. There were more knocks at the Labour Party than at the Tories. You would think it was our Act. Eventually, there was agreement to set up a committee to co-ordinate action against the Act locally. I can't say I felt any upsurge of faith in its prospect of going places. Once again I consider that's realism, not defeatism. We shall see.

13th, Friday: There isn't a great deal of industry in Islington and what there is is tending to contract. The pressure for space is enormous, mainly to fulfil those desperate housing needs. On the other hand, it is clearly desirable to retain some industry in the area. It helps the balance of the community and enables some local people, at least, to live near their work and make an indirect contribution to easing London's rush-hour travel chaos.

Pollards of London is in Highbury Grove. The firm does shopfitting work, metal architecture and so on. I spent the morning looking around the factory, talking to the directors and to many of the 300 employees, quite a few of whom are my constituents.

This afternoon I visited the New Islington and Hackney Housing Association offices and then toured a number of properties in the area owned by the Circle 33 Housing Trust. These non-profit-making outfits are valuable in supplementing the housing efforts of the over-burdened Council. But they have run full tilt into the property speculators in trying to acquire sites or houses they can renovate and let at reasonable rents. I learned of one group of houses in the Mildmay area of my constituency that was snapped up by a 'shark' for £24,000. Ten per cent deposit was paid, contracts were exchanged, and inside six weeks the houses had been resold for £45,500. What a way to make a living. Julian Amery, the Housing Minister, has just said the Government won't take any special measures to curb rising house prices because 'we do not regard housing as a commodity in the same way as shirts and food'. He claimed Government action would only curtail the supply. The case I just quoted proves the absurdity of his remarks. The speculator's only interest was in getting those houses back on the market and making the fastest possible buck.

My housing tour had to be cut short so that I could get to my evening 'surgery'.

Our Party rooms are shabby and dilapidated, although two or three volunteers have recently been busy with paint brushes, smartening up the exterior a bit. The rooms are let to us at a peppercorn rent and it is likely that they will eventually have to come down due to redevelopment.

They aren't much of a place to invite constituents to come to. I think it high time that MPs had an office and secretary, paid for by the State, working in the constituencies. It would be very much in the interests of constituents. It would aid communications, providing the secretary was not used as a barrier to prevent people who needed to see their MP from doing so. I doubt if each individual MP would merit this fullscale facility. But it could surely be arranged on a shared basis. Obviously, there would be problems but Islington's three MPs could well share an office and secretary at the Town Hall. The trouble is that in Britain we are determined to have our democracy on the cheap. Then we profess to be shocked by its imperfections.

Tonight several people were already waiting at the rooms when I got there. I dealt with a widowed pensioner having difficulty with her electricity bills, a lady in dispute over National Insurance contributions, another widow, this time making allegations against a doctor and a hospital in respect of her husband's death, and with several housing cases.

By then, it was 8.30. The waiting room was empty. I realised I had only stopped for a cup of tea since lunchtime. I was due to meet a deputation from the Highbury Hill High School Parents' Action Group. They were just arriving as I nipped up the road to the pub for a quick refreshing half pint with my Party treasurer, Jack Walker.

I was back in less than 10 minutes. I told the parents I couldn't support selectivity. They promised to give full consideration to the compromise proposals advanced by the ILEA members. It was bound to be an inconclusive meeting but we talked amicably enough for about 50 minutes and I feel I may have helped ease the situation.

There was an anonymous letter in the post this morning addressed to my wife, Pat, at our home. It said: 'Just come out of a mental hospital and killed a nigger with a meat cleaver. Calling to discuss it with your husband.' We didn't take it seriously although I wondered whether to send it to the police. But I doubted whether anyone would announce in advance their visit to see me in quite those terms.

Every so often you get a sick letter of this kind. There was one recently related to the Uganda-Asian immigrant affair which has stirred quite a bit of feeling in Islington where local Powellites are always prompt to try to create maximum alarm. The letter said: 'You were elected to look after the interests of the people of Islington East. We elected you, an Englishman, to a position of trust. Today, the country, this England, is being run by the Jews and flooded out with blacks and Cypriots and both these scum races are breading like flies. Everywhere these horrible people settle they drive out their white neighbours to make room for more of their own kind. This is all right for most MPs. They have their own farms – we, the ordinary people, have to live with these dirty noisy bastards. I hope to see the day when you MPs who have sold our country and betrayed us are *publicly hanged*. You are traitors to the British. Shame on you. – Ex-Labour voter.' Whoever wrote that knows what to do with his vote.

Anyway, no one turned up with a meat cleaver at the rooms tonight. But for all our dismissal of the letter, it left a temporary trace of uneasiness with me, particularly since it was sent to Pat.

14th, Saturday: My elder son, Miles, who is thirteen, came with me to see Arsenal's home game with Ipswich Town at

Highbury. We usually go to the home fixtures at Arsenal Stadium.

I have been an Arsenal fan since my schooldays in North London. I was on the terraces then but now customarily go as the guest of the club. I think this is about my only 'perk' of office and one which most MPs and civic heads find their respective local clubs provide. I'm just lucky that I have such a major club in the heart of my constituency. It hasn't stopped me though from raising some pertinent issues about the effects of the club's activities on residents nearby, mostly concerning noise, litter and vandalism on match days.

It's comfortable watching the game from the Director's Box. But I got more thrills behind the goal on the North Terrace where I used to stand as a lad.

17th, Tuesday: We were back in business in the Commons today after the summer recess. The first MP I saw as I walked into the Members' Lobby was George Thomson, whose appointment as one of Britain's two European Commissioners was announced last week. There is a good deal of hostility towards George because of his adamant refusal to toe the Party line on Europe. There are those who say cynically that he has reaped his reward. I think that is a blinkered view.

I have never been passionate over Europe and have always seen it as a balanced argument. For me the scales tipped against entry but primarily on the economic effects and political dangers, not arising from any deepseated principle. Anyway, I congratulated George who is a very likeable type. 'I need all the good wishes I can get,' he said with a wry grin.

The daily Question Time was already under way when I went into the Chamber. Sometimes it's more like blood sports as some unfortunate Minister is harried from the Opposition benches. James Prior, the florid-faced, fumbling Agriculture Minister, and Maurice Macmillan, miserably miscast in his present job as Employment Minister, are two who usually cop it. Today it was Prior's turn to try and parry the usual string of thrusts, mainly on price increases.

I sat in my usual place, one row from the back and just about in line with the Despatch Box on which the Front-bench Party spokesman customarily rests his notes while addressing the House.

I used to sit further from the Speaker's Chair but here I feel more sense of involvement. MPs have no fixed places but it pays to keep to the same spot. It helps the Speaker to identify you if you are trying to 'catch his eye' to get into a debate or ask an unscheduled question.

Willie Hamilton, the Labour MP for West Fife who is best known for his abrasive criticism of the Royal Family, sitting next to me, said: 'It's just like coming back to a monastery. Same old prayers.'

The Prime Minister answers questions for 15 minutes every Tuesday and Thursday. Today the atmosphere was lacking as though no one was properly limbered up for the fray yet. Heath didn't have a lot of trouble although it is recognised that he has improved his handling of Question Time immeasurably since he took office. It is far more difficult to rattle him these days and even his frequent evasions are increasingly skilfully camouflaged.

We moved on to the main debate of the day about the Common Market summit meeting which Heath is about to attend with other Heads of State. Harold Wilson's taunts and wisecracks provoked Heath into several interventions although he left it to Sir Alec Douglas Home, the Foreign Secretary, to make the opening speech for the Government. He muddled through as usual.

Roy Jenkins was called. Willie Hamilton had left and Roy was next to me. He made a powerful plea, not so much to the house as to Labour MPs. He entreated them not to boycott the European institutions after entry on January 1st – a threat which is there. I disagreed strongly with his vote against the Party Whip last year on the Market issue but I am inclined to have a good deal of sympathy with him on the likely futility of a boycott. I have yet to hear a really convincing case made out in favour of it.

18th, Wednesday: A sprinkling of MPs make a concession to the need to be physically fit. Well, at least they try. I endeavour to fit in one game of squash and one game of tennis each week throughout the year. There are squash courts in an office block near the House which MPs are allowed to use in the mornings for a nominal fee. I played there this morning with my regular partner Dick Leonard, Labour MP for Romford. I'm a lousy player but it's kind to draw a veil over Dick's performance. Suffice to say I won.

I was a little late for a special session of the Parliamentary Labour Party called to discuss the possibility of televising Parliament. There is a motion to be debated tomorrow favouring an experiment. It is Government-sponsored but there is to be a free vote and the outcome is very much in doubt. Last time it was debated was six years ago when a proposal to let in the cameras was defeated by 131–130.

Those who oppose the idea are largely the traditionalists and are fierce in their determination to resist this upstart intruder. The supporters are somewhat weakened by quite genuine doubts about the way TV should be allowed to operate. There is a mix of views on whether there should be continuous transmission, edited highlights, who should do the editing and how it should be controlled. How do you explain away the rows of empty seats to your constituents? Can you hope to convince them that so much of the work is done quietly in Committee? We all know too, that there are a lot of MPs who only appear for major votes and we are aware that the donkey work is done by a minority of the Members. I have heard it estimated that there are less than 100 Members – Ministers apart – who really keep the place going. Those empty benches are not entirely without significance.

I hadn't intended to speak at the meeting and two years ago wouldn't have dreamed of getting up without carefully preparing myself. But I could see that there were few would-be participants and thought I should add another voice to support the experiment. I said I doubted whether it would be in the interests of individual MPs but it was in the public interest. I had 'a shrewd suspicion we are in the 1970s'. I made one or two quips and my own suggestion for controlling the trial run. We took no vote and Party opinion was obviously very divided.

The main business of the day was the last stages of the Government's Bill to bring in charges for admission to museums and art galleries. I had a meeting, however, of the Select Committee on Expenditure's Employment and Social Services Sub-Committee.

There are a number of these Select Committees which are a permanent feature of the House. They exist, for example, for race relations, science and technology, nationalised industries. They choose and investigate a specific aspect of the area of policy they are intended to cover and end up with a report which usually makes recommendations to the Government. They have powers to call witnesses for cross-examination, including Ministers and senior civil servants, to make visits and to seek written evidence. Ostensibly, members are chosen by the House. In practice, the Whips' offices sort it out.

The Expenditure Committee is reckoned one of the most influential and is the biggest. It splits into Sub-Committees, mostly eight-strong, and comprising of four Tory and four Labour MPs. Our Sub-Committee is currently in the middle of a wide-ranging inquiry into the employment services. Our concern today was to agree on what further witnesses to hear and visits to make and to decide when we could begin to sift the evidence and draft our report. We agreed to aim to get to the drafting stage by Christmas.

A couple of constituents turned up unexpectedly to lobby me about the Uganda-Asians issue. London MPs tend to get more casual callers than their provincial colleagues. But even those people who only have to 'hop on a bus' to get to Westminster are risking it slightly. The MP they want to see may be away or deeply involved in a Committee or in the Chamber. Here and there MPs may deliberately dodge seeing people who turn up like this but I don't think that happens often. These constituents, both women, were bitterly antagonistic to all immigration and indignant at my support for the Government on this. I argued with them for quite some time and thought I made no impression. Still, although we had to agree to differ, they finished by thanking me for listening so patiently to their grievances.

I was 'paired' for part of the evening with Willie Whitelaw, the Secretary of State for Northern Ireland. It enabled me to go to my constituency to say a few words at the monthly meeting of my general management committee, the governing body of my local Islington Central Labour Party. I try not to miss these monthly meetings which are most important in helping to assess the feelings of the activists working, without reward, for the Party and in allowing them to quiz me. I made it clear to the East Islington Party which picked me as its candidate to fight the 1970 General Election that I wouldn't be a 'rubber stamp'. I repeated that to the new Islington Central Party, formed as a result of boundary changes, when it chose me as its candidate for the next General Election. But I try to keep in close touch with the Party and to give the management committee delegates, in particular, every opportunity to influence my actions in Parliament.

Consultation, of course, has to be a two-way process. I managed to get off my chest a beef about the failure of local Labour councillors and our Greater London Council representatives to keep their MPs sufficiently in the picture. Then I went back to the Commons in good time for the 10 o'clock vote on the museum and galleries charges. It was just as well I wasn't late. The Government scraped home by five votes – and I was told the Opposition Whips reckoned that six Labour MPs were absent without official 'pairs'. It looks as though we might well have beaten the Government.

19th, Thursday: I made a broadcast on the BBC World Service this afternoon at the studios at Bush House, Aldwych, on my opinions on the way the Press deals with the Labour Party's affairs.

I said that although it may be said that on circulation figures we appear to have our fair share of support in Fleet Street at election times, elections are not just won and lost then. I was concerned about the steady drip, drip, of anti-Labour propaganda and I contended that whenever the Party showed any signs of moving at all Leftwards its friends in Fleet Street became 'fair-weather, indeed'.

The debate on television was already going strong when I got to the House. Robert Carr, the Tory Leader of the House, gave the plan for an experiment his personal blessing. He made a Freudian slip when he assured the House there would be a *genuine* free vote. Labour MPs were quick to pick this up and contrast it with what they claim was a phoney free vote which the Tories had over entry into Europe. It was Michael Foot who lifted the level of the debate. He stood at the Opposition Despatch Box in that curious crouching stance which he adopts and performed with wit and great eloquence. He didn't have a note in sight. This would have made marvellous television – just the kind of thing the public is entitled to see.

I knew there would be a formidable queue to speak and had decided against trying. I wanted to get away for a couple of hours to drive to my 16-year-old daughter's comprehensive school in Lewisham where it was prize day. Susan is now a sixth former there but collected a fifth form prize for work last school year. It made a pleasant change to sit anonymously in the audience instead of on the platform.

I met Pat at the school and we left before the end. She came back with me to the House to hear the final speeches. I wanted to be sure I was there to vote. There was considerable excitement as we went through the lobbies. I can't remember when I was last in the 'Aye' lobby with so many Tories, although I think more of them were voting 'No.' But for a rare change no one could be certain how it would all end. It turned out to be disappointing. The proposal was lost by 191–165. So much for all the talk about the influx of younger MPs in 1970 having an impact. The traditionalists stretched their lead, compared with the vote on that earlier occasion. I told Joe Ashton, the Labour MP for Bassetlaw who spoke against the experiment, that it was 'a victory for bloody conservatism'. He could afford to laugh. He was cheering the outcome.

20th, Friday: A familiar down-and-out turned up at the 'surgery' tonight. Over the past couple of years I have tried unsuccessfully to help by contacting at various times probation officers in both London and Oxford, social services departments in two London boroughs and even the Home Office. He is not a constituent but used to live in the area. He has written to me from prison and from hospital. His letters are quite literate and from what I can make out his problem centres on drink.

At least twice previously I have given him cash to get him to a hostel for the night. On the last occasion he called he reeked of liquor and I refused him money because I could see how it would be spent. I tried to persuade him to go to a nearby hostel with a good reputation for helping alcoholics but he wasn't in a very receptive mood. After he had left I found a beer bottle smashed all over our steps.

Tonight he smelled of liquor but was not drunk. Again he asked for money. But I told him he would only spend it in the 'boozer' a few doors away. I gave him a personal note to get him into the hostel once before but never discovered what happened there. It seems it didn't work out. After a lot of argument he agreed to go there again and limped away on his crutch.

I always feel uneasy about passing this sort of case on but I can't operate as a one-man social services department. It seems like an almost impossible task to try and help someone who is neither willing nor able to help himself. He's no one's responsibility. But I doubt if I have seen the last of him.

23rd, Monday: My Parliamentary question to John Davies about the Cope appointment was due for answer today. But it appeared at No. 52 on the Order Paper which outlines the day's business. It only gave me an outside chance of it being reached for an oral reply, giving me the opportunity to put a supplementary question to the Minister there and then. I was in the Chamber just in case but the quiz show ended with several questions ahead of mine still to be dealt with. I got a written reply from Davies which merely said that Cope was bound by the Official Secrets Act.

Written replies which appear in the day's official Hansard report of the proceedings quite often produce valuable information but there is no comeback if you don't like what you have been told or consider it doesn't really answer the question at all. I have my further question to the Prime Minister on the Cope issue due on Thursday. But I understand that the Government will scrap Question Time that day so that the House can get the prorogation over and pack up. That means the House will be suspended and no more business can be done until after the Queen's speech opening the new session of Parliament next week. It looks like another useless written answer from Heath.

Heath reported back to the Commons on his summit meeting. There were some bitter exchanges between him and Harold Wilson. The personal enmity here is certainly not stage-managed. They give every impression of hating each other's guts on these occasions and MPs know they remain mutually contemptuous of each other in private, too.

The House began a three-days stint on the mammoth Local Government Bill but London MPs have a very limited interest in this and I had a series of meetings to get to, the first three fortunately all in Commons Committee rooms.

Firstly, I went to the monthly meeting of London Labour MPs. We spent an hour ranging over matters of mutual concern – vandalism on council estates, motorway development and the forthcoming Greater London Council elections. I had to leave before the end to go to the monthly meeting of the Labour Party's Greater London Regional Council Executive Committee. This consists of members elected at an annual conference from the constituency parties, the unions and other affiliated bodies. I was elected at this year's conference as a constituency representative and was rather surprised that I topped the poll in my section since it was my first attempt.

The Executive, chaired by Bob Mellish, the Cockney MP for Bermondsey who is also the Parliamentary Party's Chief Whip, is inclined to get itself into protracted arguments over all sorts of trivia. A good deal of it entails the old familiar Left-Right wrangling and leaves you wondering if anyone's ever heard of the Tories. Tonight was no different.

The Executive had previously set up a special committee to draft the manifesto for next April's Greater London Council election when we hope to regain political control of London. The agreed trio for the drafting committee are Sir Reginald Goodwin, Leader of the GLC Labour Opposition, Ashley Bramall, Leader of the Inner London Education Authority, and myself – there primarily to add some journalistic touches. This manifesto committee was next on my agenda for the evening. We quickly accepted a timetable and programme, prepared by the Regional Council fulltime officials. We know that whatever we produced would lead to fierce dissent on the full Executive. Indeed, I heard that a minority group has already met to plan its opposition to our proposals – which puts them well ahead of us!

Immediately this meeting was over I drove to Islington to keep a promise to speak at a tenants' association meeting. I had arranged a 'pair' for the rest of the evening. It was turned 9 o'clock when I got there and I was hungry, thirsty and rather tired.

The meeting was hardly worth the effort. I was well applauded for my remarks – mainly about prices, wages and rents. But as I answered questions from the floor it was obvious that the tenants wanted to get back to discussing what they had been talking about when I arrived – the every-day problems on their estate like the lack of a community hall, play space for the kids and the failure of lifts in the tower blocks. One chap said quite openly to me: 'You don't have to come looking for votes here. You'll get ours anyway.'

These people are affected far more by the national-level events I had talked of than they seem able to appreciate. I tried not to talk 'over their heads' but it was tough getting through.

25th, Wednesday: Every third Wednesday, Scottish questions take precedence. It's a brave Sassenach who intrudes. Today the loquacious Scots finished with their Secretary of State in time to allow one or two questions to other Ministers and I managed to put in a plea for consideration to be given to allowing pensioners to take out quarterly television licences instead of having to pay for the year in one lump.

Welsh MPs get a similar session to the Scots and there is a question time too, for the Secretary of State for Northern Ireland. Nothing for the English.

I moved on to a meeting of the full Expenditure Committee where Edward Du Cann, the Chairman, asked us to approve a couple of Sub-Committee reports for publication. Some of us were a bit concerned at official advice that these Sub-Committees are not entitled to issue their own Press releases about these reports, in advance but under embargo. It seems petty and an unnecessary inhibition of the rights of MPs. Du Cann, a former Tory Minister, ex-Chairman of his Party's Organisation and a man with wide City interests, is a very smooth operator. He didn't want us to make a real issue of it but he had to agree that we could come back to it in the new session of Parliament – assuming we are all reappointed to the Committee by the full House, which is something of a formality.

My next date was at a meeting of the Employment and Social Services Sub-Committee where we cross-questioned representatives from the National Union of Students. We were especially concerned with their views on careers advice and the relationship they thought necessary between Government, industry and the academic world in order to improve the matching of people and jobs. Digby Jacks, the red-bearded NUS Communist President came over very well but I felt we could have gleaned most of it from the written evidence the NUS submitted.

26th, Thursday: Parliament was prorogued today. That means a complete shutdown until next Tuesday's State Opening of the new session. I didn't go. I knew there would be a formal announcement by the Speaker of the Royal Assent for the out-standing legislation from the present session, that he would then read a brief prorogation Queen's Speech outlining what the Government has been up to and that those MPs daft enough to be around could trot up and shake hands with him before de-parting. It seemed like a good ceremony to miss.

Tonight I went to the Highbury Hill High School prize-giving. I had to tread with care since it was an open secret that the Chairman of the School Governors, Mrs Irene Chaplin, also Deputy Leader of ILEA, has been at loggerheads with the Headmistress, Mrs Majorie Butcher, over the ILEA proposals for the school's future. I had promised to be non-political and stuck to that. I gave a short address, mainly about 'the irrelevance of jargon'. I said the experts – politicians, lawyers, economists, civil servants, educationalists and so on – should stop creating con-fusion by their gobbledegook language. Everything went off smoothly but I ran into some strenuous lobbying from parents over the coffee and cakes later.

27th, Friday: The 'surgery' took about 90 minutes and was mostly housing cases. One very pleasant woman, suffering severely from over-crowding, said: 'I can tell you, whether you manage to help me or not, a lot of us around here think you are doing a good job.' It was genuine and nice to know. But it was somewhat offset by a disabled constituent who called to complain about the new rent increases and said he had been to see me a year ago about a different problem which was still unresolved. As far as I could remember, the Council had looked into his particular difficulty and found it could not help. He clearly didn't give me any marks for even trying and thought even less of our Council. If he had been a bit less aggressive I would have been more sympathetic.

I left to call on a pensioner constituent who had written to

me. I had previously managed to get this elderly lady an increase
in her social security cash and this time she wanted help in getting a housing transfer. She had a lively mind and a tongue to
match. She reads plenty of newspapers and watches all the news
and current affairs TV programmes with interest. Moreover, she
would skin Heath alive if she could get hold of him. She puts to
shame a lot of the disinterested younger folk with their lazy
lament of 'Why should I care? All you politicians are the bloody
same.'

30th, Monday: I ploughed through a wad of documents about
the proposed new Parliamentary building which will give us,
among other things, much-needed offices for MPs and secretaries
in Bridge Street, just opposite the Palace of Westminster. My
office now is in Abbey Garden. It's too far from the Chamber to
make it worth using much at all. Instead, I do most of my work
in the Commons Library. But I should certainly use a more
conveniently located office.

The Services Committee, a Commons Select Committee, has
reported in favour of going ahead with erecting the new building
as designed by the winners of an architectural competition. The
Committee's report is due to be debated soon but I have heard
that Julian Amery, the Housing Minister, is none too keen on
the project. I have read the Committee's report and that impression is confirmed by the oral evidence he gave.

I was approached by Mrs Evelyn Denington, the Labour
Opposition's Deputy Leader on the Greater London Council. She
is extremely hostile to the plans and the GLC has lodged some
formidable objections. She seems to feel the scheme should be
killed and has sent me all the details of the GLC viewpoint which
appears to unite the authority's members, irrespective of party
politics. That being so it clearly needs looking at. Things can
sometimes slip through Parliament without adequate attention,
although the Select Committee did a great deal of probing. Evelyn
Denington is to fight my constituency of Central Islington at
next year's GLC elections, hence her link with me.

I certainly wouldn't want to prevent an early end to the archaic
conditions in which MPs work but there seems to me to be good
reason to be apprehensive.

Heath, the CBI and the TUC are still at it tonight at Downing Street, trying to sort out the pay and prices situation. When I hear the late night news bulletins on these occasions, I sometimes think about the journalists covering it all. People often ask me if I miss Fleet Street after so many years working there. I got a good deal of enjoyment and a hell of a lot of frustration out of it. I certainly wouldn't have enjoyed 'doorstepping' the Downing Street talks and bashing out my copy when the participants had all cleared off to bed. And I am always able to give an entirely unequivocal reply to that question and say: 'I don't miss it one little bit.'

31st, Tuesday: I had a gallery ticket for the House of Lords to hear the Queen's Speech firsthand. MPs ballot for places. I have been previously and I think this will be enough for me. It's quite a spectacle, however. The Lords was packed with red-robed peers and life peeress members of the so-called Upper House. The other peeresses were all aglitter with jewelled tiaras and colourful sequined evening dresses worn with long white gloves.

A couple of Tory MPs from the shires sitting behind me filled in a few minutes waiting for the Queen to arrive by chewing over Tory constituency procedure for choosing Parliamentary candidates. One, who was retiring, explained that his local Party gave a lunch for those candidates shortlisted to succeed him – and, of course, for their wives. 'Don't like it really. Seems as though they want to see how you eat and watch your table manners. But it's better than having the poor girls on the platform like a damned mannequin parade,' he said. We have our selection difficulties in the Labour Party but at least we don't drag wives into it.

The Queen read her 'most gracious speech' as though her Crown was weighing her down which it probably was. The speech itself, written by the Government, mentioned the crop of legislation to come which we knew about anyway and contained the usual collection of carefully-drafted platitudes.

When this little bit of antiquated pageantry was over the Parliamentary Labour Party met for a quick look at what the speech meant and how it should be handled in the six days of debate on it which lay ahead. The Opposition can put down amendments and very largely dictate the pattern of debates on this occasion.

Harold Wilson said that after today's general debate, opened by himself and Heath, we would go on in turn, to industrial relations and unemployment, housing and land, prices and agriculture, poverty, and would then end with the crucial economic situation. I made a mental note that I would try and get into the argument on this last day.

The House got down to business this afternoon. First the Speaker, Selwyn Lloyd, read the Queen's Speech all over again. It was a ridiculous but customary waste of time. The speech had been available in the Vote Office, where we MPs get all our official documents, for several hours.

Next two Tory backbenchers moved and seconded the 'loyal address' with traditionally non-controversial speeches aimed at going down well in their respective constituencies. It's one more bit of Commons nonsense that could be abandoned with no sense of loss at all. Harold Wilson began with the usual thanks to the two Tories for their remarks and said it wasn't just formal congratulations he was offering. Willie Hamilton, sitting next-but-one to me, caused some mirth by calling out 'Of course it is.' If Harold heard, he tactfully ignored it.

It wasn't an easy speech for the Labour Leader to make. The tripartite talks on inflation overshadow everything and Heath, on the inside, had a distinct advantage in debate. Furthermore, our Party couldn't appear to want to wreck the talks nor to be telling the unions what to do.

Harold went well enough until he challenged Heath to a General Election. It was a legitimate thing to do but it simply didn't come off. The Tories were all shouting 'Lincoln' – a reference to the Labour Party's reluctance to give way to pressure from the pro-Market Dick Taverne and move the writ which would bring on the Lincoln by-election caused by Taverne's defection and resignation from the Commons. Jeremy Thorpe and his handful of Liberals, fresh from last week's Rochdale by-election success at our expense, were beside themselves with glee.

Heath was able to give the House 'a full report' of the talks in detail. He was blinding them with science until Joel Barnett, the accountant MP for Heywood and Royton and one of our Front-bench spokesmen on economic affairs, asked him point blank if he was now prepared if necessary to implement a statutory prices and incomes policy despite all he said to the contrary in the past. Heath blustered his way out of this but it was a difficult patch for him. He didn't want to give a straight 'Yes' while the talks with the TUC were still alive. But it was the honest answer and the whole House knew it.

November

1st, Wednesday: Dick Leonard phoned to switch the time for a game of squash and to let me know he had just slapped in an amendment to the Government's motion for today about arrangements for private members' business. He expected a division and I said I would make sure I was there to support him.

Dick's Romford seat is affected by boundary redistribution and he has been looking unsuccessfully for another for some time now. His pro-Market views aren't helping him. If he doesn't make it at the next election the House will lose an excellent MP and I shall lose both a Parliamentary friend and a squash partner.

He made a brief but well thought out speech today, pointing out that the Government had assigned twelve days for private members' Bills and eight for private motions in the new session. He said the previous Labour Government provided sixteen days for Bills and four for motions – occasions when there is a debate but no ensuing legislation. He rightly claimed that the Bills are far more valuable for the welfare of the people. But the Governmen Chief Whip, Francis Pym, came to the Despatch Box to insist that the motion should go through unamended.

Dick called for a division. I joined him to act as a teller. On official divisions, two Government and two Opposition Whips stand outside the voting lobbies counting the votes. This was a spot of Backbench enterprise so our Whips were not involved. The Government had played safe by making it an official Whipped vote for Tory MPs and won by 128–78. But it was a very respectable tally against them.

Reg Prentice, the East Ham MP, is our main spokesman on industrial relations and made a cogent and reasoned speech on the subject in today's main debate in the Chamber. He is well liked and respected in the Parliamentary Party. His dignified resignation from the last Labour Government in order to campaign more freely for overseas aid is remembered and stands him in good stead. But he has managed to rub some members of the Left-wing Tribune Group up the wrong way lately, mostly because of his surprisingly tough criticism of the dockers who went to jail in the summer dispute. There were a few rumblings of dissent from his MP critics during his speech today which underlined this.

The annual elections for the Shadow Cabinet are under way and I reckon Reg's vote will rise substantially. But a turnover in his support seems likely. He is an anti-Marketeer but seems sure to pick up votes from pro-Marketeers this year in an atmosphere of decreasing bitterness on this issue. On the other hand, some of the Left-wingers seem sure to desert him.

Tonight I went to Islington where a 'standing room only' meeting of my Party workers discussed the plans to reorganise education in the borough. Both Irene Chaplin and Evelyn Denington were on the platform as ILEA members and the meeting was chaired by Jack Straw, the former National Union of Students' president, who is now an Islington councillor and a member of the ILEA himself. This was one of those occasions where my presence was not necessary but where I was anxious to listen. It was not the kind of meeting to reach conclusions. It tended to be dominated by schoolteacher members who obviously had particularly strong feelings. There were some forthright contributions of real quality and I doubt if many local Labour Parties could stage a better argument on this matter of deep concern to so many of the people who attended.

2nd, Thursday: The new Liberal MP, Cyril Smith, winner of the Rochdale by-election, took his seat in the Commons – all 23 stone of him. It is difficult to gauge the significance of his appearance. It obviously reflects an element of the 'plague on both your houses' attitude of many disenchanted electors to the major parties and can't be shrugged off. But most Labour MPs see it as primarily underlining the impact which a colourful and well-known local personality can have in a by-election. And Smith certainly had the media going for him in a big way.

There was a good deal of interest in the performance of Tony

Crosland during the Queen's Speech debate today. He has managed to shake off much of the old Gaitskell revisionist image and undoubtedly remains high on the list of potential future Labour Party leaders. He certainly helped himself in the debate by pitching into Peter Walker, the oh-so-slick Environment Minister, in a way that really ruffled his feathers. Walker didn't like it all, not least when Crosland dubbed him 'What can I do?' Walker – a scathing crack using a quote from Walker in a recent interview he gave about soaring house prices.

I had to miss tonight's Parliamentary Labour Party meeting to attend the first of our fullscale drafting sessions for the GLC election manifesto. We dealt with the entire planning section but it took $3\frac{1}{2}$ hours non-stop discussion and I wasn't sorry to get away for a quick beer afterwards in the Strangers' Bar – 'Strangers' because it's the bar to which MPs can take their guests.

I got home in time to see on television that the tripartite talks at Downing Street had collapsed and it looked as though a statutory freeze was on the way. Overall, it seems as though the Parliamentary session ahead is going to be another bitter dog-fight between Government and Opposition. It promises to be an exact reversal of the roles in 1966 when the Labour Government introduced a compulsory prices and incomes policy and was opposed all the way by the Tories. If, however, we play it sensibly and don't attack the principle we can emerge fairly well. We are fully entitled to claim that no policy involving pay restraint can be supported in a situation where the Government of the day has given most help to the better-off and has pursued a consistent policy of union-bashing.

The only real surprise in all this is that the power workers have settled their pay demand. They appear to have wrenched far more than the Government would have liked from the Electricity Council yet Heath should be relieved that they have avoided a head-on collision with this industrially-powerful group of workers at such a crucial time.

3rd, Friday: The Queen's Speech debate dragged on but most Parliamentary eyes were on Downing Street where the Cabinet was in emergency session so that Heath could decide just what to announce to the Commons on Monday. I went to the BBC at

Broadcasting House to record a broadcast for the 'Week in Westminster' programme about the breakdown of the tripartite talks.

I had quite a lively argument with Tory MP Barney Hayhoe. Hayhoe came into the House in 1970 as I did and is both able and moderate which makes it difficult to score off him. I think we had a pretty even set-to.

Before we started another Tory MP, Kenneth Lewis, turned up in the same studio. Just then Hayhoe got a message he expected that 'P.M. would like a word with you'. Tory MPs were on tenterhooks, waiting for an anticipated reshuffle of Government jobs and Lewis's eyebrows shot up quite noticeably. We explained to him that 'P.M.', in this instance, was just another BBC programme.

I drove from the BBC to Islington for the 'surgery'. I was there with about an hour to spare and spent it in the Canonbury Tavern where, over a beer, I worked on my next column for 'Labour Weekly'. The once-a-fortnight column is the only regular journalism I do at the moment. It's unpaid and somewhat time-consuming but it's a very useful platform indeed.

4th, Saturday: Pat and I took our two boys, Miles (thirteen) and David (nine), to Islington for the borough's bonfire night display at Highbury Fields in my constituency. The Mayor, Patsy Bradbury, went to the microphone to announce that she was about to light the bonfire. She told the very large crowd to bring their guys up to the front if they wanted them to burn on the huge pile of wood. She mentioned I was there and one young fellow called out 'Why not put an MP on it.' He was standing a few feet from me and I could see he wasn't joking. One of my Party workers shouted to him 'Trotskyists burn better' and he scowled back and said no more.

I learned during the evening from Albert Baker and George Barnard, two of our veteran councillors, that I had been expected at the previous night's meeting of the Islington Branch of the National Federation of Old Age Pensions' Associations of which I am honorary president. I was to have made a speech and they wanted me to make a presentation to the 600th member signed on. I was both sad and annoyed because I had carefully entered a date in December in my diary and had not been told of any change, and also because the pensions problem has disturbed me greatly since I got into Parliament. I really do believe that our old folk are entitled to spend their twilight years in reasonable comfort, without penny-pinching and being subjected to a multiplicity of means tests. However, these slips will happen. I can only write it down to genuine misunderstanding.

There are some positive things you can do about issues like pensions from the Opposition backbenches. You can keep the pressure on. Just about a year ago I founded the local Federation Branch. It is now the biggest in London.

Quite a few pensioners contacted me because they noted, mainly from the local Press, that I was showing an interest in their problems and raising some of them in the Commons. One or two of them, in particular, set me thinking about mobilising them in Islington so that they had a collective voice. I wrote to the National Federation headquarters, called my own public meeting at the Town Hall, invited every local organisation I thought might be concerned to take part, and used the local newspapers to urge individual pensioners to turn up. I got about 80 people to that first meeting. Officers were elected on the spot – with Albert Baker, formerly a Mayor of Islington and once a well-known lay negotiator for the London busmen, as chairman. The Branch was well under way.

Albert told me that 160 people were at the meeting I should have attended. I agreed with him that it would be sensible to write a letter to the local papers explaining to the pensioners why I didn't get there and congratulating the Branch on its membership achievement.

5th, Sunday: The long-awaited Government reshuffle of Ministers was announced tonight. From what I heard on the radio news there was no major surprise. It was very much musical chairs with Ministers switching jobs. Opposition MPs will be far more concerned about the results of the election for the Shadow Cabinet which will be announced on Wednesday.

6th, Monday: This was the day of the freeze. The Chamber was as full as it is for Budget Day.

Heath looked thoroughly miserable and there was little of the familiar arrogance as he ploughed through his statement outlining the events during the final round of the tripartite talks prior to the breakdown. He went on to disclose the 90 days statutory standstill on prices and wages – by now regarded as a foregone conclusion. Harold Wilson made it clear that we would oppose the proposals but the most vitriolic attack came from behind Heath, from his own Benches. It was Enoch Powell reminding the Prime Minister of his pre-election pledge of no statutory wage control and asking if he had 'taken leave of his senses?' Even by Powell's standards, the stab-in-the-back was savage. Some of our MPs lapped it up a bit too readily, bearing in mind the source.

There was a forest of would-be questioners trying to get at Heath. Most like me were unable to do so but Roy Jenkins was called with devastating effect. 'Has he,' he asked Heath 'now abandoned his constantly reiterated view that a statutory policy could only make inflation worse in the long run or does he now regard the short term situation that he has produced as so disastrous that he cannot afford any longer to think about the long run?' Heath waffled but he really had no answer to that one.

The Queen's Speech debate resumed in the Chamber but I went to a meeting of London Labour MPs to hear from a deputation of trade unionists who are fighting to keep their London Transport jobs. Then I got down to a study of both the White Paper and the draft Bill on the freeze – a Bill with the weird and wonderful title of 'Counter-Inflation (Temporary Provisions) Bill'. I spent some time working out a speech in the hope that I am called in tomorrow's economic debate.

That Jenkins counter-punch was still being discussed in the bars and the tearoom. It went down with a bang. Meanwhile, the Shadow Cabinet met and apparently decided to table a so-called 'reasoned amendment' to the Government Bill which will get its Second Reading on Wednesday. No one is sure whether the Bill will be dealt with throughout by the whole House because of its crucial importance or whether it will go to a smaller Standing Committee for detailed scrutiny in the usual way. Just in case it goes 'upstairs' to a Committee, I dropped a note to Bob Mellish, the Chief Whip, volunteering to serve. I'm sure there will be a lot of our Members with the same idea.

7th, Tuesday: Quite a few Labour MPs are disturbed by the Shadow Cabinet plan for allout attack on the Government freeze. They accepted the 'reasoned amendment' stressing the failure of Tory policies but some of them backed the previous Labour Government's compulsory policy and fear they may be steam-rollered into rejecting any kind of incomes policy by the strident Tribune Group MPs. Bob Mellish has had to smooth down quite a few of them to maintain a united front. Several of these worried Members sought my viewpoint as I sat in the Commons Library this morning going through my post.

This wasn't the only issue causing anxiety. The Parliamentary Labour Party meets tomorrow to consider whether we should boycott the European Assembly at Strasbourg. The MPs who talked to me about this, including a couple of former Ministers, seemed to think it would be a futile gesture. I retain all my doubts about Market entry but I have so far, been utterly unconvinced by the case against sending a Labour delegation to the Assembly. My pre-occupation, however, was to prepare for Question Time since I had questions tabled to both Heath and Macmillan, the Employment Minister.

Macmillan's No. 2, Robin Chichester-Clark dealt with my question which concerned working days lost through strikes so far this year. The figures are appalling and I said so. The Minister was extremely uncomfortable, especially as Reg Prentice joined in from our Front Bench.

My P.Q. to the Prime Minister proved worthwhile. I managed to wrap one up which clobbered both Heath and Powell together. Heath looked a trifle puzzled when I began by assuring him that 'even though he may have taken leave of his senses, we wouldn't want him to regain them on the basis of the dangerous policies advocated by his Right Honourable Friend from Wolverhampton who stabs him in the back with such regularity'.

I went on to ask: 'Would he nevertheless answer the question he keeps avoiding? When he fought the last General Election on a policy which expressly rejected statutory wage control why has he now taken this action? Is it not a fraud on the electors?' Heath gave a fairly rambling reply about the necessity of the standstill. Several of my Labour colleagues told me they were pleased that I had shown our disapproval of the Powell approach.

We moved on to the last of the Queen's Speech debates – that on the economy. Members who want to contribute to debates usually drop a note to Selwyn Lloyd, the Speaker, in advance and I had done so. There are no guarantees though. He appears to have a system of his own for picking speakers which takes into account the number of times you have spoken previously in the session and probably allows for special interests, too. But there is a feeling among younger Backbenchers that the dice is somewhat loaded against them and that seniority of service is unduly recognised. Privy Councillors always get preference. It wouldn't be so bad if some of these old stagers weren't so longwinded. They seem to delude themselves that the world is hanging on their every word or maybe they just love the sound of their own voices. They tend to forget other people in the queue.

I have just signed a motion calling for the Speaker to be allowed to limit Backbench speeches to 15 minutes each. I doubt if it will have any effect. But I always aim at 10 minutes and reckon that 15 minutes is ample for anyone, other than in very special circumstances.

The Speaker wasn't prepared to commit himself when I asked him about my prospects tonight. He said he hoped to get everyone in who had asked to speak. In the event, I think he managed to do so.

I got my 10 minutes at around 8 o'clock. It's not easy to work up a punchy style in a sparsely-populated Chamber. The public gallery was full but you don't notice that when you are speaking.

Anyway, I got in some fierce stuff about the Government's record and its treatment of the unions. And I dubbed Ted 'the Dodger of Downing Street' for his policy changes. I claimed he had 'betrayed his mandate'. It should read quite well in my local Press and the one thing I did make sure of was that I got on record my continued support for a prices and incomes policy under a Labour Government which provided the right economic and social background. That's something I don't think can be said too often by too many Labour MPs because there are enough people in our own ranks who knock the concept with noisy consistency.

Michael Foot wound up the debate for us. His first 15 minutes was magnificent. It was both wounding and witty at the expense of the Tories opposite. But he got involved in a heated clash across the Despatch Box with Heath about just who did cause the breakdown of the Downing Street talks and I felt he rather lost his way, although it was the kind of bitter exchange that will doubtless capture some headlines. Jim Prior, who has just been switched from Food and Agriculture to become Leader of the House, ended for the Government. The final speech is always the worst to make. Opposition MPs want their last chance to harry. Members on both sides have usually wined, dined or maybe just had a beer or two. At any rate, they are that bit more truculent. Prior's speech was abysmal. And he sat down early which led to a rowdy incident as a Labour Backbencher tried to pinch the last couple of minutes of debate before the 10 o'clock vote. The Speaker wouldn't have it and there was an inevitable argument on points of order. It had all got a bit theatrical. What was certain was that we would lose the vote. And, of course, we did.

8th, Wednesday: The Parliamentary Labour Party meeting to discuss sending delegates to Strasbourg was a pretty dismal affair.

Frank Judd, formerly one of Harold Wilson's Parliamentary Private Secretaries and now a junior Frontbench spokesman on Navy affairs, started with a reasoned speech against participation. Denis Skinner, the 1970 intake miners' MP from Bolsover, was quick to support. Denis has forged a reputation as a cheeky chappie in the Chamber but today he was too strident and too long to do his case much good.

Douglas Jay, a Right-winger on most issues is passionately anti-Market, and poured out his scorn. But easily the most telling speech for a boycott came from that roly-poly figure Ray Fletcher. He has an intimate knowledge of Europe, spends a lot of time there and was listened to with respect.

Three main points emerged from the arguments for a boycott:

that it might embarrass the Tories who would be thwarted from sending many MPs if Opposition Members were not there to balance the number of Westminster absentees;

that the gesture would impress on the Community that we really do mean business with our renegotiation line;

that the Party conference has told us to keep away.

Pro-Marketeers like John Mackintosh and Willie Hamilton saw

a boycott as futile. So did one avowed anti-Marketeer, Geoffrey Rhodes, though his contribution lost quality through quantity. There were harsh words between Willie Hamilton and George Thomas who accused each other of being offensive. George, following on, told Willie he hadn't been offensive but 'I can be and if you'll be patient I will be.' It was a good crack which brought laughter but the meeting had deteriorated sadly.

One unusual intervention came from Ron Hayward, the new Party general secretary and an old friend. He was understandably trying to raise the status of Transport House, the Party headquarters, and to put a view for the National Executive Committee which is responsible for the Party outside Parliament. He warned of the danger of a gap between MPs and rank-and-file Party workers if we failed to take conference decisions seriously.

The trouble is that this particular conference resolution was woolly and open to various interpretations. Not that Ron anyway, suggested that conference decisions should be binding on the PLP.

There was a certain unreality about the debate. I don't really see our activists believing a new gap is opening up between them and MPs simply because we send a delegation to Europe, particularly if it consists of mostly anti-Marketeers. As for the general public, they couldn't care less about this. This issue will only be as significant as we choose to make it. Unfortunately, some people are determined to stir it up, to turn it into a new Market cause celebré. If they achieve that aim, it can only be to the detriment of the Party as a whole.

The meeting was tetchily inconclusive. Now the new Shadow Cabinet must meet to work out its recommendation to put to another fullscale Party meeting shortly. I tried to get in towards the end of today's debate but was unsuccessful. I have rarely used my Labour Weekly column to deal with matters of current Party controversy but I think I will do so – and the message will be 'Keep it cool'.

I got in twice at Question Time this afternoon. I pushed again for quarterly TV licences for pensioners – this time the rejection by the Posts Minister, Sir John Eden, was a lot less emphatic and gave cause for some hope – and also quizzed the Civil Service Minister, Kenneth Baker, about the effects of the freeze on civil servants' pay.

Between phone calls, I was in and out of the Chamber to hear
bits of the opening speeches by Tony Barber, the Chancellor,
and Harold Wilson on the Second Reading debate on the Counter-
Inflation Bill.

But the interesting event of the afternoon was the outcome of
the Shadow Cabinet elections. My forecast that Reg Prentice
would improve his position proved to be an under-estimate. He
topped the poll along with Shirley Williams, the Shadow Home
Secretary and a leading pro-Marketeer. Merlyn Rees was the
newcomer to be elected. He has impressed as our Northern
Ireland spokesman and got my vote. He is a moderate on most
things but is also an anti-Marketeer.

There was a tie for twelfth and last place between Peter Shore
and John Silkin. It looked like an eliminating ballot. John came
into the tearoom while I was there and someone quipped: 'Canvassing for votes already, John?' He had the perfect answer. He
said he had already told Peter Shore, a fellow anti-Marketeer,
that he would withdraw in his favour.

The only casualty was Barbara Castle. It was no surprise. Her
ability is unquestioned but her erstwhile Left-wing friends have
never forgiven her for her industrial relations White Paper 'In
Place of Strife' which roused the unions to so much anger. And
the Right-wingers, who never did more than tolerate her as a
Minister, now view her anti-Market views with distaste.

The overall result of all this is a fillip for the pro-Marketeers,
particularly because of the restoration to the hierarchy of Harold
Lever, who quit the Front Bench over the Market along with
Roy Jenkins. The vote for Shirley Williams is another boost for
them.

In the Grand Committee Room in Westminster Hall, the
architects for the new Parliamentary building were showing
slides of the project. The working environment will be de-
lightful for MPs and I'm not against a sauna and swimming
pool. But there seemed to be an incredible amount of open
space and I get the feeling that the whole thing is that bit too
extravagant.

I nipped over Westminster Bridge to County Hall for a meeting
of the Greater London Labour Party's publicity sub-committee.
It was mainly concerned with the layout of the election address
for next April's GLC contest. I had to leave before the end to get

to Islington for a public meeting called by Holloway Ward Labour Party.

Holloway is in George Cunningham's constituency but will be in mine after the next elections, electors willing, because of the boundary changes. One of my innovations has been to hold public 'report-back' meetings around the Wards at which I tell constituents what has been going on in Parliament and let them fire their questions. I have tried to kill the claim that you only see your MP at election time. It's not easy to get people to this kind of political meeting but I have had anything from 25 to 60 turn up.

Holloway has been a somewhat moribund Ward politically. There is a great deal of redevelopment taking place which hardly helps to keep any community spirit going. So I wasn't too surprised that the church hall meeting was down to about a dozen people, including the handful of activists who run the Party there. It contrasts sharply with the customarily well-attended meetings of other local Wards.

The chairman, Ted Holroyd-Doveton, a local councillor, told me they usually meet over a pub and that ensures a better turnout. Still it was probably just as well that the audience was small as I had to dash back to the Commons for the vote against the Counter-Inflation Bill.

9th, Thursday: I left the GLC election manifesto drafting committee, meeting in a basement interview room, to go to the usual Thursday evening session of the Parliamentary Labour Party. 'I'll only be a few minutes,' I said as I left. I should have known better.

The first 25 minutes of the Party meeting was a fiasco. It was spent in a childish, often churlish, squabble about whether John Silkin should be allowed to withdraw in favour of Peter Shore as twelfth man on the Shadow Cabinet. They are both anti-Marketeers and it was a pro-Market group which sought to cause an upset. They tried to argue for a new Ballot of the whole Party to fill the place, obviously in the hope that a pro-Market candidate would oust Shore.

Fortunately, the bulk of the MPs there recognised the damage that could be done by this manoeuvre succeeding. It certainly seemed to me like a pretty tawdry attempt to tilt the weight of the Shadow Cabinet still further towards the pro-Marketeers who would then secure a top-level proposal to the Party to send our delegation to Strasbourg. It was one more example of the bitterness which is creeping back over this non-issue.

I paid a quick visit to the Russell Hotel for a reception given by the National Union of Bank Employees for some of their European counterparts. Maurice Macmillan, the Employment Secretary, had been and gone when I got there but Reg Prentice was there.

NUBE had been suspended from the TUC for refusing to deregister under the Government's Industrial Relations Act. I had been invited to the function before that break took place but would have gone along anyway. Several of the union's senior officials are old friends and would personally have preferred to come off the register if their members had allowed it. But the membership voted otherwise and these officials are thoroughly disenchanted at the poor treatment they contend they got from the TUC which they claim bullied them rather than sought a compromise.

13th, Monday: In the post today there was a letter from the taxman. That is inevitably depressing. I took a sharp drop in income when I entered Parliament – that's not a complaint, just a statement of fact. Since then I have been unable to put anything by and but for persuading the Inland Revenue to wait for a due payment, I would recently have had to draw on past savings to meet their bill.

As a family we certainly don't live extravagantly. We have very little time for hobbies or entertainment outside the home, we don't spend much on drink and I am a non-smoker, our kids go to State schools and our last three annual holidays have been relatively inexpensive ones in Wales and Scotland. True, I changed my car after I got into Parliament and bought Pat a small secondhand one. Without it, she would find it virtually impossible to run the home and also manage the teacher training course she is pursuing. I don't rate this as luxury spending. I can only echo every housewife's lament: where does the money go? I earned quite a bit extra from regular newspaper articles in my first two years in the House but that source of cash has largely dried up. My only permanent outside income now comes from the CPSA and is modest enough.

MPs' overheads can be quite heavy even though some secretarial and other expenses, like travel are met. There are all sorts of subscriptions and donations which have to be paid. But back tax has been my problem. I didn't put enough by to meet the tax on those extra-Parliamentary earnings during the first two years. Paying it off has temporarily swallowed up all the benefits of the rise in MPs salaries to £4,500 a year. If I'm having trouble, with a sizeable income, it certainly shows just how grim it is for those on low pay or fixed incomes in this inflationary whirl.

14th, Tuesday: An anonymous caller phoned this morning, wanting to give me confidential information about the way some computer training schools exploit immigrants.

He had seen a newspaper report about a question I asked in the House about this yesterday. He had firsthand knowledge of one of these schools. He said they advertised all over the Middle East and in many other countries for students, implying that they could secure them entry to Britain. Would-be students would take a ridiculously simple aptitude test and be asked to send £90 to book a place on the course. The cash was non-returnable.

Often they were refused entry and that was the end of their cash. Those who got here mostly registered for the course, clocked in for part of the day, then worked at part-time jobs. They paid a total of £350 to £420 by instalments and if they lagged the school, which retained their passports, would report them to the Home Office making it plain they were no longer studying at all. Even those who sought to take the course properly were unlikely to finish up with a recognised qualification and had scant prospect of a job in the computer industry.

I arranged for this informant to meet me at the Commons. He said he could provide documentary evidence to back his story. It certainly sounded a racket that should be investigated and exposed.

The Government duly got its guillotine motion today to ensure that the Counter-Inflation Bill goes through the House rapidly. We went straight on to deal with the Bill in a Committee of the whole House. It meant that all the MPs form the Committee and have the right to speak and move amendments. In practice though, only 50 or 60 MPs at the most were likely to do much work on it.

I wanted to contribute tonight because I expected other commitments would keep me from the Chamber for part of the following two days and make it more difficult for me to keep adequately in touch with the progress of the Bill. Just before I spoke at around 8 o'clock this evening, a Powellite Tory, John Biffen, made a vitriolic attack on his own Government for deviating yet again from Tory principles in introducing the Bill. Biffen is uncannily like Powell in both his style of speech and his mannerisms, even down to details like holding no notes and clasping and unclasping his hands, almost as though wringing them in anguish. It is as though he has modelled himself in hopeful preparation for donning the mantle when the time comes.

In my own contribution, I backed the Opposition line that the Bill should not be activated for a time to allow for a resumption of the tripartite talks. An amendment of that kind had no chance of success but allowed for a wide-ranging debate. I made a couple of worthwhile constituency points about land speculation and rent rises in Islington, accused the Prime Minister of again leading the British housewife 'up a blind alley' on prices and claimed that the Government was keen to pass every law it could to 'keep the working people in what they regard as their rightful place in society'. But I got over again my support for a voluntary incomes policy under a Labour Government.

15th, Wednesday: My informant called to see me about the computer schools. He produced a whole wad of letters which he had apparently filched from the school to back his contentions. He appears to be revealing a decidedly shady operation. I was tempted to say I would take the lot to a newspaper and get them to lift the lid right off. But I think I shall first write personally to Ministers and arrange to see them informally. That way I can find out just what effective action is possible on an official basis.

The Counter-Inflation Bill churned on its way. I had discussed with the CPSA its implication for Civil Service pay and I made a brief intervention in the debate to remind the Chancellor, Tony

Barber, that civil servants, whose pay is decided by the system of 'fair comparison' with similar outside jobs, are always behind in the annual pay queue and the freeze means they must lag for even longer. I warned that unless this was taken into account in working out the next phase of the policy there was a danger that the whole 'fair comparisons' scheme would be repudiated by the unions. It seems that there is, indeed, some risk of this.

19th, Sunday: I wrote my Labour Weekly piece about the European Assembly. I reread it about four times before I posted it. I wanted that 'play it cool' message to come across and I didn't want to provoke a backlash that would only make things worse. I think I got the balance about right but it is bound to upset some of the hardliners.

20th, Monday: All around the House there are indicator screens to tell you who is speaking in the Chamber.

I was working in the Library when the motion congratulating the Queen and Prince Philip on their silver wedding anniversary came on. Heath, Wilson and Thorpe spoke in turn and I had no doubt I was missing nothing but the orthodox. Then I noticed Willie Hamilton's name flash up on the screen. I looked into the Chamber to see what scorn he was pouring on the monarchy this time. In fact, he began by joining in the congratulations. But that was just a prelude to an attack on the 'sordid greedy commercialism of the event which money-grubbing loyalists are busy cashing in on'. I not only share Willie's basic contempt for the monarchy as an institution but also his sentiments about the money-grubbers.

A Tory called him 'the big bore of West Fife', as he chuntered on. Willie's back is broad. Moreover, he knew he would get some headlines. But there is a time and place for everything. This wasn't it and that Tory was right. Even our side of the House was bored and clearly thought it all too contrived. Willie tends to overstep the mark in bitching about the Royals and gets far too personal. It's good for publicity but doesn't make the case. On the other hand, most Labour MPs are too scared of constituency reactions to voice much criticism at all of the monarchy and all its trappings. It is totally incompatible with democratic socialism yet during last session's debates on the Royal pay rises when Willie Hamilton was ill and I moved most of the amendments objecting to the Government's handling of the issue, there was precious little support from Labour MPs. Some of the Left-wingers who might have been expected to chip in were conspicuous by their absence.

The Counter Inflation Bill completed its short sharp Commons progress tonight. There was a Government majority of 29 on the Third Reading – 292 votes to 263.

But the main interest was focused on what will happen on Wednesday when the Government's new rules on Commonwealth and European immigration are to be dealt with. Tory Backbenchers are restive at what they consider will reduce the status of White Commonwealth citizens from Australia, New Zealand and Canada, below that of our new Common Market citizens. Sir Max Aitken's Daily Express campaign on this is undoubtedly biting.

We have a two-line Whip on it and will oppose the Government, although I trust on somewhat different lines from the Tory rebels. But the Government will apparently impose a three-line Whip. That means our would-be absentees will not be able to find Tory 'pairs', so it will be an effective three-liner for us as well. Defeat on it could hardly bring down the Government. But there is a lot of speculation about the outcome. Even so, we have had these false hopes raised before and our own people don't really expect the Tories to lose the vote.

21st, Tuesday: Officially opening an open space may seem a bit odd but that's what I did at St Paul's Shrubbery in the constituency this morning. It does have significance in Islington which is so sadly starved of land for open space or building.

Questions to Jim Prior on food prices always get pretty rough and his successor, Joe Godber, now the Food and Agriculture Minister, won't have it any easier to judge from today in the House.

But it was an all-woman incident that got rowdiest. Mrs Peggy Fenner, the newly-appointed Minister for 'the shopper', at Godber's elbow, had to answer a question about consumer matters from Mrs Sally Oppenheim, the Tory MP for Gloucester, who was widely rumoured to be her rival for the Ministry job.

The House can be cruel on occasion. And Sally Oppenheim, whose carefully-coiffured appearance adds a touch of brittle glamour to the dowdy Tory Benches, was the immediate butt of Labour ridicule.

'Congratulate her,' they chanted at Sally as she stood up to put her question. She was temporarily taken aback and bemused by the racket. And Labour wag Bill Price, MP for Rugby, yelled out to loud laughter, 'Give her a kiss.' Even Tories were grinning. I doubt if anyone heard the question or Mrs Fenner's reply. I know I didn't.

Schoolboy frivolity? Undoubtedly. But a bit of light relief is no bad thing. The House overall, is a serious enough establishment to allow for these moments of 'banana skin' humour. Indeed, some Members take themselves far too seriously with very little cause.

I had a PQ to Heath on the Order Paper about further talks with the TUC and CBI on inflation. It wasn't reached so I went to the Table Office to stick in the same question again for a fortnight's time. The clerks there get hogtied by all sorts of technicalities and said that since it was down for today and I would get a written answer, it couldn't be tabled again before this had appeared in Hansard, the official report.

Eventually, we settled for a different word formula which asked almost the same thing. It's triviality like this which is so irritating. You can usually find a way round it. It is tempting to consider launching a campaign to reform the system but there are so many facets and it would be a remarkably long haul for no more than marginal effect. Most MPs, regardless of Party label, are very conservative in these matters and I can use my time more usefully. That, I suppose, is what most Members who are critics of archaic rules and regulations, think about it which is why the absurdities go on . . . and on.

The Parliamentary Labour Party's Economic Group had its annual meeting to elect officers. The chairman had been Dick Taverne whose ability in this field was recognised. But it only took a moment to replace him with Joel Barnett, who was unopposed. It was reminiscent of the way Roy Jenkins's job as Shadow Chancellor was rapidly filled by Denis Healey. It's all a measure of political indispensability and there's no one it doesn't apply to.

22nd, Wednesday: My scheduled time for leaving home for the House this morning was wrecked by a succession of phone calls, including one from the BBC which required a dash to do a broadcast.

Still, I managed to keep a squash date, picked up my post at the Commons and moved on to a lunch for Labour MPs given by the Israelis. The Israel Ambassador was there – and so, understandably, were a couple of Special Branch men. I had to leave before the coffee and speeches to get to Westminster Central Hall to speak to CPSA members in London for the afternoon lobby of Parliament by the TUC on pensions. I explained to them the ground rules for lobbying MPs and said a few words about the issue itself.

Over in the House it was chaotic. I wandered around the Central Lobby and precincts for some while trying to find Islington pensioners' representatives and some Post Office union people who had written asking to see me. I eventually caught up with the Islington people but never located the trade unionists.

Eventually, I went out to the St Stephen's Entrance where hundreds were held back behind the barriers. The police called for any more Islington folk and half a dozen trade unionists – not those I was seeking – were allowed through to see me. I must have spent 20 minutes or so chatting with them and when I got back inside I found I had missed an unexpected division in the Chamber – on, of all things, the Bill to provide the £10 so-called Christmas 'bonus' for pensioners. I hadn't realised before that division bells don't ring outside the entrance. Still, it was only a two-line Whip and I learned I wasn't the only one to be caught out in the muddle that was going on.

It's not accidents like this that bother the Whips' office. It's the regular and calculated offenders. They make difficulties for everybody.

Meanwhile the Shadow Cabinet met. It cautiously backed away from a showdown on sending a delegation to the European Assembly. It is to recommend that the PLP doesn't send but reviews the situation in a year's time.

It's a sloppy solution but it defuses a dangerous Party situation and I'm not unhappy. It pulls the rug out rather from under my Labour Weekly piece that will appear at the week-end saying 'cold logic' demands we should send MPs. But I have qualified that by insisting that it is far more important to avoid tearing ourselves to bits over it – and anyway, who can pretend the Labour Party runs on cold logic. Not that I would want it to really.

It was an historic Parliamentary occasion when the new rules for Commonwealth and European immigration were voted on. The Government was convincingly beaten – by thirty-five votes. Seven Tories came into the Lobby with us and forty to fifty abstained. It left Heath in a real predicament. He will have to redraft the rules to take account of the views of his defectors. Even before the vote was announced there was a tremendous racket and atmosphere of anticipation in the Chamber. By now, only the size of the majority was a surprise. Labour MPs yelled 'out, out' at Heath. Harold Wilson threw out the inevitable challenge, implying resignation was necessary and knowing full well nothing of the sort would happen. Heath duly parried the thrust but he looked grim, careworn and badly shaken.

Our MPs were understandably euphoric in the emotive atmosphere. We rarely get a voting victory in the Commons. But it won't look quite so marvellous in 24 hours or so when it has simmered down and we all appreciate more clearly the role played by Sir Max Aitken and the White Commonwealth lobby.

24th, Thursday: The British-American Parliamentary Group ought to be important but isn't. So far as I can see it provides scant opportunity for MPs to get know much about the current American scene that you can't read in the papers. No doubt, a minority of long-serving Members gain from it but today was the annual meeting and I can only recall one letter from the Group – an invitation to a reception for visiting Senators – since the last annual meeting. Jim Callaghan seemed anxious to give it a 'kiss of life' and Lewisham Labour MP Roland Moyle, who has taken over as secretary, should help this revival.

But some of the all-Party overseas groups which abound at the Palace of Westminster seem as often as not to be joined by peers and MPs who simply expect a trip out of it and have no concern for the politics which ought to be involved.

The Speaker, Selwyn Lloyd, has regular lunch parties in his State rooms for small groups of MPs, working through the list. I went along as his guest today. Most of the table talk was about inflation. But we also got on to the possibility of a time limit for Commons speeches. There was no all round agreement on either subject.

This afternoon the North London teachers – the National Union of Teachers in Islington – lobbied us for support in their argument with the Education Minister, Margaret Thatcher, over their frozen London allowances. I had booked a Commons Committee room and arranged for the other Islington MPs to join me there. The teachers had trouble getting in but there must have been 70 or 80 in the room eventually. They were justifiably angry at the treatment by the Government but one or two of them just didn't like politicians. Stop.

25th, Saturday: Finding the opportunity to read is a major problem. A sizeable chunk of the week-end has to go on this, encroaching considerably on what I wistfully regard as family time. The political weeklies, the local Press, the daily and Sunday newspapers seem to load me down with print every Friday, Saturday and Sunday. I could get by with reading very little but why be in politics if all you want to do is get by?

Then there's the usual morning mail. Today's contained Greater London Labour Party material to be scanned before meetings on Monday, a weighty Expenditure Committee report and various other documents which needed some attention.

It really is well nigh impossible to conscientiously brief yourself adequately on the wide selection of issues you are expected to vote on, if not to speak on. You have to work on the principle that when in ignorance or doubt you follow the official Party lead, usually determined by the Front Bench specialist on the more obscure matters. It's imperfect but there's no workable alternative.

This afternoon Pat and I took the two boys to the Islington Central Labour Party's Christmas bazaar. People are wheedled and cajoled into producing goods for sale for months in advance by Mrs Agnes Seeley, our social secretary and a dedicated Party worker for many years. There's always an air of crisis in advance but it goes off well on the day and makes a fair profit for Party funds. This year was no exception and we finished about £100 to the good.

27th, Monday: I picked up 16,000 leaflets from the printers to be distributed to my constituents. There should be enough for every house, if not household, to get one. The leaflet takes the form of a 'half-term' report on my activities to the people who sent me to Parliament. The leaflet is a considerable personal 'puff' but I can't spare my own blushes in this sort of exercise. It also advertises my advice bureau and Labour Weekly, has a 'join the Party' appeal and gives a good plug to Mrs Denington, next year's GLC candidate. The Party was keen on the idea when I suggested it and volunteers will deliver the leaflet.

The House was discussing new measures to give compensation to people hit by planning 'blight' but I went to the Greater London Party's monthly executive meeting in an upstairs Committee room and then settled down to yet another drafting session on the GLC election manifesto.

38th, Tuesday: The Commons Tearoom is regarded as a good place to sound out opinion – and informally to express it. Some highpowered canvassing has gone on there over the years.

It's a funny sort of place. Labour Members use it rather more than the Tories who tend to gather in greater numbers in the Smoke Room where alcoholic drinks are served.

In the Members' Tearoom, we sit at one end and the Tories at the other. There's very little inter-Party fraternisation over the teacups whereas it's by no means unusual in the bars. Not that there's a great deal of mixing between Members of the political parties. The Members' Dining Room sees a similar division to the Tearoom. It's just that buying drinks at the bar pushes people together by accident, not design, and occasionally conversations strike up.

There are, of course, always exceptions to the rule. I can think of at least one Tory who only appears to drink with Labour

Members. Indeed, the story is told that after he had been in the House for about six months, one of his fellow Tories stopped him in the corridor and said: 'I say old chap, would you like to "pair" tonight?'

Five of us – all Labour MPs – sat in the Tearoom this morning over cups of coffee and talked over the Strasbourg situation. There was indignation at the generalisation being peddled that MPs, unlike local Party activists, are out of touch with the feelings of their constituents. It's true, mind you, of some MPs but not of the majority of our Members.

Indeed, as someone pertinently pointed out, MPs are often more likely to know constituency feeling through advice bureau work, through regular contact with Party workers and – very important – through their postbags. Obviously the extent of the physical contact varies according to the geography of the seat. I am well placed with a London constituency and home and can be with my electors and Party activists far more frequently than, say, my Welsh or Scots colleagues.

Overall, the charge which amounts to one of neglect is decidedly unfair. But there are enough backsliders to give the determined critics a peg to hang their case on.

29th, Wednesday: This afternoon the new Expenditure Committee met for the first time since its belated reappointment for this session. The Committee could and should have been operating for the past couple of weeks but last session's chairman, Edward du Cann, was elected chairman of the Tory 1922 Committee, his Party's influential Backbenchers' setup. He therefore quit the Expenditure job. This appeared to cause delay. So did the attempt to sort out the Tory delegates for Strasbourg. I got to the meeting a few minutes late and the new chairman had already been elected. He was Sir Henry d'Avigdor-Goldsmid who seemed to me a singularly uninspiring choice. I gathered he was not opposed which meant the so-called 'usual channels' had operated between the two main parties to carve up the choice. The 'usual channels' is Parliamentary shorthand for the Whips acting on behalf of the Party leadership.

I protested at the meeting at the delay in reappointment which led to our Sub-Committee postponing visits and scrapping meetings for the cross-examination of witnesses. The best one can hope is that it won't happen like this again. I also raised the highly controversial subject of the possibility of televising the Committee proceedings. I told the new chairman that I would write to him setting out the case and proposing a motion.

He didn't seem to take too kindly to a contentious matter arising at his 'baptism' meeting in the chair and there were rumblings of discontent from several Members, including at least one on our side. There is clearly a view that the recent vote of the House against admitting the cameras to the Chamber closes the issue.

But the work of a Select Committee is very different. It justifies a different approach. I expect to be in a minority on the Committee but a lot will depend on who turns up on the day it is debated. Even if I did succeed it would require a further debate and a vote by the whole House before the scheme could go ahead. The odds are heavily against but it's worth a try.

On the floor of the House Jack Ashley, the Labour MP for Stoke on Trent, spoke from our Front Bench, opening the debate on the thalidomide children. Jack has done tremendous work on this tragic affair and has been a tireless champion of the disabled. He illustrates the impact that a Backbencher can occasionally achieve and his Front Bench appearance was a deserved touch.

Jack has his own major handicap. He is completely deaf. He was already a Member when this personal disaster happened and thought he would have to give up politics. But he was persuaded otherwise, learned to lip read, and with the help of his wife, has soldiered on to great effect.

In fact, his deafness does give him a slight political advantage. He is listened to more attentively and sympathetically and, as he pointed out to the House, it wasn't much good trying to interrupt him even if someone wanted to. When Ministers reply to his frequent questions they usually try to talk back, looking at him and mouthing their words carefully to help him lip read. It's one of those small human extras which crosses the Party divide. Although I missed most of his speech because of the Expenditure meeting I was glad to learn that he did a first-class job.

I also went to a short special meeting of London Labour MPs to arrange a deputation to Margaret Thatcher in support of the teachers' allowance. It was just about the best attended meeting of its kind I have been to and the teachers should be encouraged by this show of genuine interest in their case. There was a National Union of Teachers' official there to deal with any points we wanted clarified.

Later the House debated juggernaut lorries. The Government cautiously refrained from fighting this Labour motion expressing opposition to allowing bigger lorries into Britain whatever the Common Market requirements. Heath is still smarting from his defeat on the immigration Order and doesn't want to risk another rebuff – quite a possibility on this emotive issue which many Tory MPs also feel strongly about.

30th, Thursday: We were told tonight that there will be another attempt to upset the Government's European plans. The Parliamentary Labour Party will next Tuesday demand the postponement of Value Added Tax for at least a year. There is some hope on our side that we shall again attract Tory rebels. No doubt we shall pull in a few but I can't believe that on this one there will be enough to worry Heath.

December

1st, Friday: When it's very cold or very wet, fewer people call at the Friday 'surgery'. Tonight it was both and the customers were few which was convenient because Pat and I wanted to go on to the Mayor of Islington's annual reception at the Town Hall.

But there was one disturbing case of domestic difficulty. The wife – kicked out of her home by her husband – was unable to obtain maintenance from him despite a court order. She came to me in tears and near-hysteria. I managed to calm her down and explain to her how to get free legal advice locally. But I may have to bring in the Social Services Department at some stage.

The Mayor's reception was a pleasant occasion. In between the socialising and dancing, I collected one speaking engagement, one request to put a Parliamentary question and a batch of queries to answer myself. In addition, I paid up my Labour Party tote money – to the Mayor, Mrs Patsy Bradbury, who happens to be my constituency Party collector. You soon get used to mixing business and pleasure on evenings like this.

2nd, Saturday: I knew that most of tomorrow would have to be spent working on that voluminous GLC election manifesto ready for the final drafting meeting on Monday. So I wanted to be as up-to-date as possible with everything else.

There was an enormous bundle of post – it varies in size to a considerable extent – and I spent most of the morning sorting it out so that I would be prepared to dictate replies first thing on Monday morning to my part-time secretary, Doreen Wright.

I drove to Highbury in the afternoon with Miles and saw Arsenal beat Leeds United 2–1. On the way home I stopped off at the BBC to record an interview on the failure of the Government's Counter-Inflation Act to deal with increases in rents in furnished private properties – 'an astonishing omission', I called it.

Pat and I spent the late evening at a social held by the Labour Parties in Bromley. As a Labour activist in the borough for many years and chairman of the local Labour Party there for four years until I went into Parliament, I like to maintain some links with my old friends in the area.

3rd, Sunday: Trying to lick that manifesto into shape took about seven hours – minus about 30 minutes teabreak. The Party's London research officer, Peter Walker, joined me for much of the time.

4th, Monday: First came that session of dictation, clearing about three dozen letters, then a car dash to the House for the final manifesto drafting committee meeting. That went on through lunch which turned into a glass of milk, and even then I had to leave shortly before the end.

I saw Sir Geoffrey Howe, the Trade and Consumer Affairs Minister, and David Lane, the Under Secretary of State for the Home Office, privately in Sir Geoffrey's room at the House. The issue: the computer schools scandal. Howe felt it was primarily a matter for David Lane, who looks after immigration policy at the Home Office. I agreed but I stressed the need for action. I passed over photostat copies of the documents from my informant to help with the background. I told Howe how I had come by them and he was a trifle embarrassed but both Ministers felt they should 'accept service'.

Lane promised to start investigations going. I told them my informant thought of going to Enoch Powell but being an immigrant didn't go through with that. They agreed with me that Powell would have tried to make much of this situation and I said 'So could I.' I pointed out that I could have gone straight to a newspaper and got a major probe going but I felt that I should first give the Government a chance to stop the racket. They were grateful for that although they accepted that at some relevant stage I shall probably want to speak out. Indeed, Howe took my point that there might come a time when it would be helpful if I did so, perhaps naming the company in the House. They promised to keep me posted. I don't expect much development this side of Christmas. I telephoned my informant to let him know that things are slowly moving.

5th, Tuesday: I had Question 21 on the Order Paper to the Employment Secretary, Maurice Macmillan. When he and his Ministerial team handed over questions to the Prime Minister after 45 minutes, my PQ had still to be reached. It seemed ridiculous.

There were two reasons. Some of the early questions on the Order Paper were linked with other similar questions appearing lower on the list. The Minister took them together for answer and that gave those MPs a chance to 'jump the queue' in getting in their supplementary questions to him. Coupled with Macmillan's faltering and longwinded style of reply, it cut out questions from many of us who might otherwise have reasonably expected to be called.

I had a PQ to the Prime Minister too but that appeared fairly low on the Order Paper so there was little chance of getting in on that one. It was one of those frustrating and time-wasting occasions which is virtually unavoidable.

The House debated the Opposition call to put off the 'evil day' of VAT. The arguments have all been so well rehearsed over the months that I listened to very little and certainly felt no urge to take part. Any Opposition would feel the need to continue to harry the Government on a major matter like this. It's part of the job and it's right to do so. It is a means of maintaining Parliamentary scrutiny and moreover has a political propaganda value. As a member of the Party's Economic and Finance Group, I would have joined in if asked. But our side apparently had no shortage of speakers. And as a member of last summer's Finance Bill Committee team I heard enough about VAT then to see me through for quite a while. In the event, the Government had no trouble in securing its majority. Only three Tories abstained and none voted with us.

*　　　*　　　*

C

6th, Wednesday: About two dozen of us from the Parliamentary Labour Party's Economic and Finance and Trade and Industry groups went to the Japanese Embassy to discuss that country's trading relationships with Britain.

The Japanese Ambassador came over as an able and knowledgeable diplomat in the face of some pretty tough questioning, particularly from some of our MPs with constituencies where employment has been affected by Japanese imports. He pointed out that contrary to general belief, the trade balance – taking into account 'invisibles' (services like banking and shipping) as well as the flow of goods – has been consistently in Britain's favour.

Some of his Embassy colleagues were somewhat less convincing than the Ambassador but it was an interesting session followed by a pleasant buffet lunch.

I was back at the House in good time for questions at 2.30 p.m. Indeed, I waited outside the Chamber with other MPs while prayers were held as I wanted to be in my place as soon as Question Time was under way. As an agnostic, I never attend prayers in the Chamber. I have no objection to those who want to doing so but I share the view of quite a few MPs who feel it is a nonsense that several minutes of Question Time is lost each day while the Speaker's Chaplain conducts this ritual. Today there were about ten Tories and one Labour MP taking part. That's a measure of the demand.

Prayers over, the doors opened and the rest of us streamed in. Up in the gallery, the public were admitted. The situation has something in common with that at the cinema where most people scramble to get out at the end of the performance before 'God Save the Queen' is played.

I was fortunate at Question Time for a change.

Frank Allaun, the Left-wing Labour MP for Salford, who batters away ceaselessly at the Tories on housing, attacked them over the latest council housing completion figures which make this year seem likely to be the worst for new homes since at least 1963. Tony Crosland, our Front Bench Shadow spokesman, weighed in, too.

I managed to catch the Speaker's eye as he let the questions on this important disclosure run on a bit. I told Paul Channon, the new Housing Minister, that the figures made Ministerial boasts that they would speedily clear the slums 'look like the sick joke of the 70s – a sick joke at the expense of those in need of decent homes'.

I had my own question listed at No. 31 and this time it was reached without difficulty. It concerned speculative office building in central London and, naming a specific example, I accused the Government of 'pandering to profiteers'. Channon looked suitably embarrassed, especially as Chris Tugenhat, Tory MP for the Cities of London and Westminster and one of his Party's more progressive Backbenchers, came in to ask him to switch the emphasis from office building to homes.

Our Expenditure Sub-Committee had a significant encounter. Mrs Renee Short, the red-headed Labour MP for Wolverhampton North-east, is about as partisan a chairman as you could have. The Tories would like to get rid of her. But there are times when her approach is valuable in a strictly non-Party fashion. Today she had summoned the top civil servant from the Department of Health and Social Security to tell us why there had been no Departmental response to our report on private practice and its effect on the National Health Service which was published eight months ago. The Permanent Secretary was most apologetic and explained that there was to be a White Paper published soon on the subject. But he got a severe dressing down in one of those all-too-rare examples of Backbench MPs insisting that the Executive treats them with respect – or else.

The rest of our session was spent in examining witnesses from the National Council of Women and from the shopworkers' union about employment problems.

7th, Thursday: I was among a small group of Labour MPs at a lunch given by the Advertising Association ostensibly to discuss consumer affairs but, at least in part, to sound us out on the Party's thinking about its policy towards the advertising industry. The AA people stopped some hostile questions but I think both sides learned a bit.

Heath had just started answering questions when I got into the Chamber. I went on to a meeting of the full Expenditure Committee. I had sent my letter as promised to the Chairman setting out the case for televising some of our proceedings and I had added my motion to cover the point. Apparently the Chairman discussed the matter with James Prior, now the Leader of the House, who felt that although TV in the Chamber had been ruled out his mind was not closed in this further respect. So the motion was put on the agenda for next week's meeting and we passed on to other matters.

Tonight Arthur Davidson, the lawyer MP for Accrington, Dick Leonard and myself, went by car to Uxbridge to give a hand in the eve-of-poll campaigning to get Manuela Sykes, the Labour candidate, returned. I had never met her but Arthur knew her from her Liberal Party days. 'I never thought I would ever be out canvassing for her,' he said. By the time we had negotiated some considerable traffic jams and found our way from the main Committee rooms to a Ward Committee room it was getting on for 8 o'clock. Still we got in our stint of 'knocking up' – trying to ensure that those listed as Labour supporters as a result of past canvassing, actually turned out to vote. We were in a good Labour council estate but one irate elector, who had just been disturbed by a small boy singing carols, told me in no uncertain terms: 'I've already voted. You must know that. So 'oppit.'

I got home about 11.30 p.m. and was called up by the BBC about an hour later to join in a 'hook-up' phone debate on 'live' radio with Chris Tugenhat, for the Tories, and Lord Byers, for the Liberals, on the consequences of the results at Uxbridge and Sutton and Cheam, where the other by-election of the night was on.

The broadcast was in advance of the declaration of the results. I didn't attempt to hide that it would be a serious rebuff for us if we lost Uxbridge, a marginal seat where a small swing would give us a gain.

Pat was watching TV in the lounge. She told me Denis Healey said roughly the same thing for us on television, though perhaps slightly more cautiously.

I was pretty demoralised when the actual results came in. I had said on the radio that defeat would mean some heart-searching for us and would spur us into a more positive policy-making effort. That was certainly no understatement.

8th, Friday: On the way to the 'surgery' I called in for half-an-hour at a Westminster reception for senior officers of the Socialist

Group of the European Parliament, given by George Thomson, now styled the EEC Commissioner Designate. All the talk, during my brief stay, was about the by-elections and the need for the Party to get a grip on itself. Several of the more sensible pro-Marketeers there talked about the effect of the by-elections on next Wednesday's Parliamentary Party meeting about the Strasbourg delegation. I accepted that the results are likely to aid the case for sending our MPs and that yet another negative gesture will damage our stock still further in the country. But the pro-Marketeers have been told that Lord George-Brown intends to try and speak at the meeting. George – together with a few other over-zealous Europeans like Willie Hamilton, Charles Pannell and George Lawson – could well turn out to be the kiss of death and there was considerable anxiety about their possible interventions.

I still rate it a ridiculous issue to have an internal fight on but it seems there is no way around it; I feel I should try and speak as a 'soft' anti-Marketeer who favours sending delegates. Nor can I support the Parliamentary Committee's flabby compromise of suspending a decision and meanwhile sending a delegation, simply to liaise with the Social Democratic Group within the Assembly. George Cunningham, who has also voted consistently against the Tory entry terms, has a sensibly-worded amendment down for the meeting, calling on us to take up our entitlement to send delegates 'to try and moderate the adverse consequences of membership of the Community during the period of Conservative Government'. I told him earlier in the week that I expected to support this line and the events of the past 24 hours confirm me in my view that it is right to do so.

10th, Sunday: One small postscript to the by-elections that occurred to me. The newspapers scarcely gave a line to that Parliamentary clash over the housing figures just 24 hours before polling. True, the Guardian ran a front page story the day before. But imagine what Fleet Street would have made of the situation if it had been a Labour Government. Those figures were news and it's hard to accept that political judgment is not involved in burying them in such delicate electoral circumstances.

Tony Crosland's speech to the London Labour Mayors' dinner

was very much in line with my views at the moment. He said, in effect, that there has been so much Tory-bashing that policy has been neglected. He's right.

But I hope he can inject some urgent and radical thinking into our own approach on housing and land for which he has some direct personal responsibility. Of course, he's not on the Party Executive Committee, the main policy-making body. I just doubt whether he will seek to go far enough in an area where drastic reform would not only be morally right but would be politically popular. There aren't too many policy fields where we can point to that kind of dual advantage for being as ruthless in the interests of the people we represent as the Tories have been for their followers. This is one such field and we shouldn't hold back.

11th, Monday: The GLC election manifesto meeting, held in a Commons Committee room, dragged on for $3\frac{1}{2}$ hours. When the dust settled, the manifesto could be seen to have been approved but not without many misgivings. There will have to be quite a bit of rewriting to take account of dissident views but at least it doesn't have to go back to the full Executive again.

There was an anguished discussion on whether we could commit a future Labour GLC to refuse to operate the abhorred Housing Finance Act in line with the view of the London Region's last annual policy conference. Our paragraph in the draft dealing with this was undoubtedly sloppily worded. But we got a slightly amended version through after a good deal of squabbling. It committed our GLC candidates to continue the fight against the Act if elected and no more. Any other verdict would have caused an immense public row, with the resignation of key Labour figures from their candidatures, and would have wrecked our hopes of recapturing political control of London. It seemed to me that even those who sought the more militant outcome were not unduly displeased that they were overruled.

Even so, I remain unhappy with the overall document. I was supposed to lend a crisp professional touch. I haven't been able to do so to my own satisfaction, partly because the whole thing covers too much ground in too much detail, partly because of the very limited powers of the GLC which is hemmed in by national government, but most of all because it has been a ridiculously rushed job. If I ever get involved in this exercise again, I shall insist on a far greater say about the length of the document and about the timetable.

16th, Tuesday: The Society of British Motor Manufacturers gave a lunch for a few Labour Members at their Hyde Park headquarters. I appeared to have been invited because of my interest in industrial relations but spent much of the lunchtime discussing the problems arising from juggernaut lorries.

I had to dash off early from the lunch to get to the House for questions. I had tabled one to Sir Keith Joseph, the Social Services Minister, asking him to take action on proposals in the latest Task Force report 'Left in the Cold – final evidence of the suffering of pensioners in cold weather'. I told him it could have been called 'freedom to freeze' and attacked the lack of progress since the 1971 Task Force report 'Old and Cold in Islington'.

Sir Keith said he was discontented about the ability of any government quickly to reach all those entitled to benefit. But he stuck to his line that the real problem was 'take-up' – getting old people to apply for heating allowances – rather than lack of available cash for them if they did so.

I had fixed a quick mid-afternoon game of squash immediately after Question Time and was out of the House for about 50 minutes. When I got back I phoned home and spoke to Miles, who had been off school with a bad cough and cold. 'By the way' he said, as an afterthought just as I was about to hang up, 'the London Whip phoned. Mr Wilson wants to see you'. I told him to pull the other leg, then realised he wasn't joking. So I located Ernie Perry, the MP who acts as Whip for all the Inner London Labour Members, and he confirmed that Harold had asked to see me. I had no idea why. Nor had Ernie. I was aware that new junior Front Bench appointments were due soon but that seemed a highly unlikely reason for seeing me. I had written a lighthearted Labour Weekly piece, referring rather saucily to the Leader, and had also been quoted over the week-end in the Times and the Guardian as a critic of muddled leadership over the Strasbourg 'great non-issue'. But I couldn't imagine that those matters merited his attention overmuch. So I thought it must be something entirely different – without being able to work out what.

In Harold's room, he told me he thought we should go back to the situation that existed when Hugh Gaitskell led the Party in Opposition and have a Front Bench spokesman on information, the media and so on. He wanted me to do the job. He pointed out that there is increased interest in the Party in these matters and made it clear that he thought my general Fleet Street know-how would be valuable.

We had quite a long relaxed chat. We chewed over the Strasbourg situation and I told him I thought the Parliamentary Committee's recommendation was wrong. He defended it on the grounds of Party unity. I could see his predicament. Leading the Labour Party is a virtually impossible task.

Harold asked me not to mention that planned appointment until he announced his Front Bench changes which were unlikely to take much longer to complete.

It was only when I left him that I began to feel a bit shattered. It could well be an extremely important and exciting job with a considerable impact on the Party's image. I had certainly not expected this kind of advance after less than $2\frac{1}{2}$ years in Parliament.

Pat met me at the House soon after and I told her about it. But it was hellish difficult not to mention it to some of my Parliamentary pals and I am going to have trouble to avoid spilling the beans to one or two MPs who got to know that I had had a session with Harold.

17th, Wednesday: The Parliamentary Labour Party meeting was packed for the crucial argument about the Strasbourg delegation.

Harold Wilson turned on a persuasive performance. He avoided dealing with the merits of the case overmuch, slammed the Press for its treatment of the Party's differences, pleaded for unity and insisted that 'from today, I, for one, will have no patience whatsoever with anyone who rocks the boat. Nor will the Party in the country.'

What if the Shadow Cabinet recommendation was defeated by the MPs present? Would there be the same acceptance of a democratic decision? That was what I wondered. But I knew the answer really. There wouldn't be much hope of it. There is a relatively small group of constituency activists who would be sure to fight to reverse such a vote and would receive encouragement from the dedicated anti-Marketeers within the PLP.

Well, it won't be put to the test.

George Cunningham spoke ably, making, as an anti-Marketeer, most of the points I would have liked to advance. I was sitting next to Roy Jenkins who argued with some passion for participation. Michael Foot wound up for the Shadow Cabinet with a speech that was far less effective than I had expected. He tried to deal with the merits of the boycott but was unable to disguise that what it all adds up to for him is not renegotiation but pulling Britain out of the EEC, come what may. Not that he actually said so; he didn't have to.

Anyway the Cunningham amendment was beaten by 134 votes to 88. I stuck to my view that the Parliamentary Committee was wrong even though Harold Wilson's speech made me think over the position again very seriously. But I reckoned it would be funking it to vote any other way.

I think our credibility in the country will suffer further short-term damage but, to be fair, only marginally, on what the public see as a non-issue. I'm not really unhappy at the result which should help to avert a very uncomfortable period of internal Party strife. On the other hand, I doubt if we'll be long finding some other wrangle.

Our Expenditure Sub-Committee heard from Clive Jenkins, that livewire general secretary of the Association of Scientific, Technical and Managerial Staffs. Clive, an old friend from my industrial reporting days, lambasted the private employment agencies. We went on to hear evidence for their 'defence' from some of the bosses of the big agencies. They were a largely unconvincing bunch.

14th, Thursday: The main Expenditure Committee took its time today before it got to my motion for televising its proceedings. The chairman, Sir Henry d'Avigdor-Goldsmid, would have preferred not to have got there at all. He said he would consult the Speaker about the propriety of the move, as though that was sufficient. In fact it has nothing to do with the Speaker.

I made it clear my motion would be put and debated. He could hardly rule it out of order since plenty of notice had been given. I could see, counting heads, that I had a sporting chance of success, contrary to what I previously expected. There were a good number of younger Labour MPs there, several of them urged by me to attend. Eventually, the vote went 12–9 my way. One of the younger Tory MPs, Dan Awdry, voted for my motion so it wasn't a strict Party lines division. Another Tory, who had to leave early, told me later that he too, would have voted for my proposal if he had been there.

Less than half the Committee was in attendance. But that's quite normal and all the members had copies of my letter setting out the case for the proposal so no one could claim it had slipped through improperly.

Now a report to the House must be issued for approval by a majority of all MPs. Sir Henry may well try and see the matter 'pigeon-holed' – which is what happened under the Labour Government – but he'll run into trouble if he does.

It was quite a nice little victory over the hidebound traditionalists who make up the bulk of the anti-TV vote and it could start a few other Committees of the House thinking of similar action. Indeed I was told that some members of the Science and Technology Select Committee may try to follow suit.

15th, Friday: The BBC asked me to broadcast on that Expenditure Committee decision about the TV cameras. I had to be careful not to disclose details of what happened inside the private meeting of the Committee to avoid any possible breach of Parliamentary privilege prior to the publication of the report on the subject.

In the Chamber there was a debate on London affairs – in particular, the cost and scarcity of land and housing. I had done a spot of preparation but there were very many Labour MPs wanting to speak and since I missed the start of the debate because of the broadcast, I decided to opt out on this occasion.

At the 'surgery' I had an eighty-seven-year-old ex-policeman call to ask about the effect of the Housing Finance Act on his rent. His landlords – a pensions trust, ironically – want to treble it and have won the first stage of the battle. I explained to my constituent how to get advice about rent allowance and agreed with him that he should go ahead with an appeal to a rent assessment panel. I said that if that failed and the allowance was insufficient to avert hardship, I would send a letter to the trust stressing his difficulties. I doubt if it would work but it might be worth a try.

17th, Sunday: There were several of the younger Labour MPs at a private party I was at tonight and the talk swung around to the familiar grumbling about the leadership and the need for new blood on our Front Bench. I wasn't going to disagree about the need for changes! But I felt thoroughly inhibited.

19th, Tuesday: The Christmas recess starts at the week-end and lasts until January 23rd. But this week's business is deliberately light. No votes are scheduled. It means that MPs with homes and constituencies in faraway places can use the opportunity to get away early. At the same time, the Government can mop up a few of the outstanding non-controversial items of legislation that are hanging about. The drift away was apparent even at Prime Minister's Question Time with far fewer Members in the Chamber than usual.

I attended the final meeting of that protracted GLC manifesto drafting committee to sort out the amendments before the document goes to the printers. And I went, too, to the annual meeting of the Parliamentary Party's Posts and Communications Group. I have a dual interest here – in the postal side because of the CPSA's Post Office membership and in communications because of a general interest in the media and my background in journalism.

Later Pat met me at the Commons and we went on to Highbury Grove School, the big comprehensive in my constituency where we had been invited to the carol service. The school has a majority of Labour governors – plus Dr Rhodes Boyson, the Headmaster, a former Tory Parliamentary candidate who is best known as a contributor to the education 'Black Paper'.

* * *

20th, Wednesday: The Speaker annoyed quite a few of us by refusing to allow more than a single supplementary question about the appointment of Sir Michael Swann as the new chairman of the BBC. I tried to get in on several other questions too and it was one of those days when I reckon I needed a red flag to wave at Selwyn Lloyd. I didn't make it. Norman Buchan, one of our Front Bench spokesmen, drafted a letter to the Speaker complaining about his gag on the BBC question and several of us associated our names with this protest.

Our Expenditure Sub-Committee finished off its cross-questioning of the employment agency bosses. There were only three witnesses this time, out of the five we saw last week. This time they put up a better show. We are still not at the drafting stage of our report and have further witnesses to see after the Christmas break.

A group of workers from Task Force, the young people's volunteer organisation, came in for a quick meeting with myself and Michael Meacher, the Oldham West MP who is a 'cert' for a Labour Front Bench job in the near future in my view. He is a specialist in the social services field who frequently throws a barrage of embarrassing statistics at the Government. The Task Force people were anxious to keep up the campaign to secure adequate heating allowances for old people and several possible courses of action were canvassed. Our visitors asked about involving the trades unions in this specific aspect of the pensions problem and I suggested they should write to Vic Feather, the TUC general secretary, sending him a copy of their latest proposals and seeking the support of the TUC General Council.

Harold Wilson has now postponed his intended announcement of the rest of his Front Bench team until some time after Christmas which he is spending in Israel. I don't know the problems which are causing the delay but its darned frustrating. I shall do some 'swotting' on the subject of the media during the recess anyway and hope he doesn't change his mind so far as my appointment goes. Not that I can see why he should.

I made a point of telling the delegates at the Islington Central Labour Party management committee tonight how I voted inside the private meeting of the Parliamentary Party on the Strasbourg issue. The Press is, of course, briefed on what is said at the PLP

meetings and on the decisions but the way people voted is regarded as their private property. I told my local Party that I
thought that on a matter of this consequence I should put them in
the picture. No one queried my vote – although it could have been
the festive spirit in the air.

I also said a bit about the heavy-handed Government action over
the 'leak' inquiry going on into the *Sunday Times* disclosure of
the Department of the Environment document about rail cuts. I
said that phone tapping and undue pressure on journalists involved had implications for the freedom of the Press and attacked
Heath for hypocrisy in advocating more open government. I
wouldn't say the delegates were greatly concerned about this one
but I had done a Press release on it so I wanted them to know
my viewpoint before it appeared in print.

We ended the meeting in rather unusual fashion. Everyone had
been asked to bring something to drink and there were 'hot dogs'
and chips as well.

22nd, Thursday: Leslie Huckfield, the bearded trendy-suited
Labour MP for Nuneaton, has been battering away in the House
on the *Sunday Times* rail cuts story. I was not in the Chamber to
hear him do so once again yesterday but the newspapers this
morning refer to him alleging a campaign of 'terror' by the
Government over the probe. That seemed a bit too extravagant.
In a Radio London interview arising from *Times* and *Guardian*
quotes of my remarks last night, I said I wouldn't regard the
incident in itself as a serious threat to Press freedom but if it
signified any sort of trend then I should take a different view
which was all the more reason for exposing the situation fully
right now.

23rd, Friday: The final pre-Christmas series of adjournment
debates took up the day. Each of the MPs who had secured time
from the Speaker was allocated a 30 to 45 minutes spot. In these
setpiece debates, Members can raise any matter not requiring
legislation and a Minister is required to be there to reply to their
arguments. It's a good opportunity to air a constituency grievance
or pursue an issue on which you have failed to get a satisfactory

Ministerial answer during Question Time. One such debate takes place for 30 minutes every night before the House rises.

But it's usual to find only the Member concerned plus the junior Minister detailed to answer in the Chamber on these occasions. That was certainly the case when I last had an adjournment debate – with only the Speaker and a few folk in the public and Press galleries for extra company.

Most MPs had left for their homes and constituencies earlier in the week and I had no reason to attend today. It was a good chance to do a spot of belated Christmas shopping.

28th, Thursday: I read in the morning papers about the arrival at Gatwick Airport of Howard Hughes, the American multimillionaire recluse. He was apparently admitted without a valid passport. I didn't see anything wrong with that, if he was able to prove his identity, though I doubt if ordinary travellers would find things working quite so smoothly for them if they turned up at immigration without that precious document.

But it did seem that Hughes had received considerable preferential treatment overall – customs and immigration officers going out to his private plane to arrange his clearance and a fleet of Rolls-Royce cars allowed out on the tarmac to pick up Hughes and his entourage.

It all contrasted sharply with the way the immigration people dealt with the American actress Jane Fonda and her boy friend a couple of days earlier. They had great difficulty in gaining entry to Britain because of their links with Vietnam anti-war protests. And a constituent of mine was recently caused much distress at Gatwick when her sister tried to gain entry from Iceland and was refused entry in a most hamfisted manner. In this latter case, I was phoned from the airport by my anguished constituent and had to chase up Home Office officials in the middle of the night. I thought I would put down a question to the Home Secretary, Robert Carr, asking him just what special arrangements were made for Hughes.

I released the text of the question to the Press Association news agency. Then the fun started. You can plug away on some great national issue and no one wants to know. Backbenchers, in particular, are of scant consequence and Front bench spokesmen often find it near-impossible to get their viewpoint across. But pick an offbeat issue like the Hughes affair and everyone goes barmy.

The rest of my day was largely spent answering newspaper queries on the phone and doing radio and TV interviews, including television news spots for both our ITN and for American TV.

It's a decidedly odd world with a decidedly odd sense of values.

31st, Sunday: I had considered writing to both Islington Borough Council and the Greater London Council to find out whether they had any shares in the Distillers Company and, if so, asking them to back the call for an extraordinary general meeting of shareholders as part of the campaign to step up compensation to the thalidomide children.

Although I have not previously played any direct role in this dispute, clearly the more pressure that can be brought to bear on the company in the interests of these tragic kids the better. Helpfully, the *Sunday Times,* in the forefront of the campaign along with Jack Ashley and the parents concerned, today listed all the major shareholders. Islington doesn't figure but the GLC is there as the biggest of all the local authority shareholders.

I whipped off a letter to Sir Desmond Plummer, the Tory GLC Leader, seeking his support for the campaign and took care to send a copy to Sir Reginald Goodwin, the GLC's Labour Opposition Leader. I let the Press know of my action, well aware that Plummer is ultra-sensitive to public opinion in the GLC pre-election period. I shall be surprised if he turns down the request especially as he knows that I have been in touch with Reg Goodwin, too.

January

1st, Monday: E-for-Europe day is no different from any other
New Year's day for most people. The evening papers and the
news bulletins indicate that thousands are not at work. There's
no suggestion that they are celebrating entry into the Common
Market, simply that many of them have that morning-after-the-
night-before feeling.

My letter to Plummer had received publicity and a keen young
man from Radio London was on the doorstep his morning to
interview me while I was still coming round – or, to be strictly
accurate, dictating letters in a none-too-fluent style after seeing
the New Year in.

Every morning newspaper has acres of space devoted to our
new European link but the country remains sharply divided on
the merits of entry, according to the latest opinion poll. This
presumably accounts very largely for the grey anti-climax which
the moment of entry has brought. So many people feel they have
been bulldozed into the Market that there is no perceptible
enthusiasm on what is really an historic occasion even if you
would prefer this page of history never to have been written.
Heath has achieved his most burning political ambition but it
has turned into a sour and jaded sort of victory for him.

3rd, Wednesday: Plummer sent his reply about Distillers to me
by hand. He wanted to release it smartly to the Press. Rather as
I had anticipated, he has committed the GLC to backing the call
for an extraordinary general meeting of Distillers shareholders
although he won't go as far as to brand their compensation offer
inadequate.

His announcement has been a bit overtaken by other developments on the Distillers front: the Chancellor's statement that the company cannot expect any special tax concessions on its compensation payments and Distillers' ill-judged retort that this means the current offer will have to be withdrawn. This can only cause more alarm and anger among the parents of the thalidomide children and is a further example of the incredibly inept and heartless handling of the whole affair.

4th, Thursday: I got a letter from an ex-GI called Joe who lives in San Diego, California.

He described Howard Hughes as 'our great man' who 'labored with time and money to help win the last war . . . for British salvation'. He had read 'where some squirts don't want him in England' – a reference to an attached Press cutting from an American newspaper mentioning my criticism of Hughes's smoothly facilitated entry into Britain.

This fellow was well steamed up. He attacked British punks who take away a fortune in American dollars through singing and dancing and picked on Tom Jones and Engelbert Humperdink. And he said of Hughes: 'Your hotels, etc., are making a fortune from him as you clip him good.' At least that point seemed valid.

Ex-GI Joe went on: 'Just to think that we bled and toiled and died, many of us in two wars in my lifetime. There was no complaints from your lousy outfit when I was put off the boat in Liverpool in World War One, in my American uniform, my whole life badly altered . . . what for? To save the lousy British Isles. I knew then that your sorry outfit is no good and not worth saving.'

I never realised before that the United States won World War One for us, as well as World War Two.

Anyway, friend Joe is an isolated critic among the comments and letters I have had on this subject.

5th, Friday: There is to be a public inquiry next week at Islington Town Hall into applications by a property company to develop some of its houses by turning them into single unit accommodation. They want to transfer elderly people living alone in other property owned by the company to these houses which are the subject of the applications. The Council opposes the applications and so do the tenants and other local residents. Hence the inquiry.

Some of the residents have sought my support. I wrote today to the Council's Chief Solicitor asking him to pass on my written views to the Inspector conducting the inquiry.

The Council, it seems, must argue largely on planning grounds related to the specific properties but I can be less inhibited. My letter questions what will happen to the houses vacated by the people transferred.

I warn that the properties may either be modernised and let off at very high rents or, more likely, sold off at prevailing extortionate prices. There will then be no genuine housing gain to Islington and it can only add to the squeeze on middle and lower income wage earners who are increasingly priced out of the area. I claim that the speculators have made enormous sums this way in the borough in recent years and suggest that if this particular property company – which has a history of frayed relations with its tenants – wishes to challenge this assertion it might care to open its books for independent scrutiny. There is little chance of that.

Islington's Branch of the National Federation of Old Age Pensions Associations met tonight at the Town Hall. I went along, after my 'surgery', to keep a date as guest speaker – the role I should have filled last November.

There were about 90 people there which is good going for a pensioners' organisation on a cold dark January night. I was there this time as a local MP rather than as Branch president and could be Party political. I didn't overdo that, however, although I lashed into the Government on prices. I spoke about pensions generally and about heating allowances for the elderly.

Then I referred to the recent cases of several old people, living alone, found in their rooms weeks after their deaths. I said that what happened in these tragic cases could well happen in Islington – a view which had been confirmed for me by social workers. I suggested the Branch might discuss the problem with the Council and other local voluntary organisations and look especially at the possibility of establishing street 'vigilante' groups to make regular checks on old folk living alone, not to intrude but just to see that they were not in difficulty. I stressed that there could be no foolproof system. But more could be done.

The best piece of news is the decision by the Distillers Company to step up its offer of compensation to the thalidomide children. There is no doubt that this has only been achieved through the growing pressure of public opinion, expressed through the Press and by the actions of major institutional shareholders. My contribution, in prodding the GLC, has been very small but I'm glad I did so. Every little helps, even though it's immeasurable.

10th, Wednesday: Sir Geoffrey Howe, the Minister for Trade and Consumer Affairs, replied to me today on the computer schools affair. It was a pretty cautious response but he pointed out that both the Home Office and the Department of Education and and Science were also looking into the matter. He couldn't see anything to justify a prosecution under the Trade Descriptions Act although he stressed that local weights and measures authorities have the statutory duty to enforce the Act and could consider any specific complaints. He did think the general question of non-returnable deposits which students are asked to make might be something which the new Director General of Fair Trading might refer to the Consumer Protection Advisory Committee 'with a view to action being taken under the powers contained in the Fair Trading Bill if it is enacted as drafted'. That's a new Government measure which Parliament will deal with in the coming session.

I shall await the reactions of the other Government Departments before I decide what to do next. I don't expect much from the DES on my suggestion that there might be a code of practice to govern schools of this kind or that control should be exercised through licensing and inspection. But I shall be particularly concerned if the Home Office fails to get to grips with the way overseas students are fleeced.

The special Communications Group, set up by the Party's National Executive Committee to look at the media, had its second meeting at Transport House tonight under the chairmanship of Tony Wedgwood Benn. This Group, of which I am a member, reflects the concern expressed at last year's Party Conference where a resolution was approved calling for a more balanced Press which could be achieved by a policy of positive discrimination towards less-favoured newspapers. It asked the next Labour Government to establish a National Printing Corporation to help struggling and prospective newspapers and to acquire plant so that it could contract out the publication of newspapers. It wanted better distribution by wholesalers and retailers, regardless of the political or religious bias of the newspapers and a wider spread of Government advertising around the Press. The resolution also claimed that the Tories have almost complete control over publishing, advertising, distribution and retailing and argued additionally, for more 'impartial controls' for TV and radio with greater opportunities for minority groups to put their views.

This Communications Group has brought together a wide variety of people with media interests in what appears to be the first-ever exercise of its kind despite the many years of bitter complaint about the way the Labour Party is treated by the media. More recently, the unions have heightened their interest in this issue. The TUC is investigating and our meeting saw strong representation from the printing unions, including the journalists, and especially from the cine technicians.

Any time a speaker wants a round of applause from a Party meeting or Conference he only has to attack the 'capitalist Press'. It gets absurdly overplayed. But it rarely fails.

Yet the case can't be lightly dismissed.

Fleet Street is fairly balanced in dividing its support between us and the Tories at election time – but only as long as the Labour Party doesn't challenge the status quo, the existing order of society. The local Press is heavily pro-Tory in its editorials in most areas. But it is mostly ready, even eager, to print news whatever the political source, and much of our difficulty in getting coverage here is a failure to recognise this and respond to it.

The meeting got down to some useful discussion which ranged over control of the Press, worker participation in running newspapers, methods of aiding poorer newspapers through newsprint or advertising levies, the desirability of a National Printing Corporation, and so on. There will have to be quite a few further meetings before we can begin to point the Party in the direction of a *policy* for the Press.

What did come through was the feeling that it is even more urgent for the Party to man the barricades on broadcasting where Tory Government decisions that will pander to their friends with commercial interests at the expense of public service broadcasting are imminent. There was great anxiety about the future of the fourth television channel.

Tony Benn cheered up the cine technicians' union people by telling them that he anticipated the Opposition making it clear in the Commons that it would not be bound as an incoming Government by decisions taken now in advance of the full-scale inquiry into broadcasting which the Party wants. This sort of statement would have serious implications for anyone intending to put cash into TV deals on the basis of what could turn out to be shortlived Tory promises.

I went on from Transport House to Broadcasting House to be interviewed on the BBC 'World Tonight' programme about the walkout demonstrations during the day by civil servants over their pay. Their action was unprecedented and far more effective than had been expected.

I ran slap into an excellent example of heavy prejudice. I don't know the politics of the interviewer, Douglas Stuart, but he clearly began from the premise that the civil servants were in the wrong and every question was designed to prove this. I got through it smoothly enough – though an explosion of anger (synthetic or real) might have been a worthwhile counter. He got me to record my support for the action – he clearly felt sure of that since I am CPSA Parliamentary Consultant – then suggested I was backing anarchy, that civil servants should always carry out the will of the Government and that they sought special treatment. It was all in that vein. I didn't complain but that's one BBC man I shan't regard as impartial in the future.

12th, Friday: There was a meeting of a few people with Press and public relations experience at the Party's London Regional Office to sort out the best way to handle the GLC election address. As with the manifesto, I became part of the team (this time just two of us) press-ganged into writing it.

I encountered a distressing situation at the 'surgery'. A middle-aged woman who desperately wanted a move and alleged harassment from her upstairs neighbours. It would have been hard to prove her charge which mostly amounted to overhead noise late at night. But her nerves were obviously on a knife-edge and she claimed she got little sleep. She told me she had been near to suicide. And she broke down and sobbed.

She had seen the Housing Department but didn't know what they were doing about her case. It didn't sound very hopeful. This kind of problem requires flexibility and Housing Departments of local authorities, which understandably have to abide by the rules or stand accused of allowing queue-jumping, don't have much room for manoeuvre if a case doesn't have the necessary paper requirements to justify action.

Anyway I told this constituent that I would look into the matter promptly and do my best.

13th, Saturday: Every so often, playing a ball game, you hit a winner that feels really good.

I can still remember rattling the crossbar in a football match with a tremendous leftfoot volley that was better than any goal I ever scrambled home. It must have been all of 20 years ago. This morning at tennis, I played the perfect overhead backhand crosscourt volley. But these occasions stick out for the enthusiastic amateur because they are rarities.

15th, Monday: Another two-hour session of the Greater London Labour Party executive. We had a long wrangle about the confidentiality of executive documents, mainly because the details of the manifesto had leaked out all over the place. Most of the discussion was too mundane to recall but when we got on to the by-election results at Uxbridge and Sutton, Bob Mellish made a punchy little statement which indicated that the Party leadership has finally realised that we have to start banging over our policies.

16th, Tuesday: The Civil and Public Services Association held a rally tonight at Central Hall, Westminster, to further their protest at the discrimination against civil servants which the Government's pay freeze entails. The main hall was packed and there were two overflow meetings. Apart from the opening remarks by the president, Len Lever, there was only one speaker – the general secretary, Bill Kendall. I sat beside him on the platform and was well applauded when introduced.

Bill gave the Government a rough time. He made it plain that the days when civil servants wouldn't dream of militancy are over for good. On the other hand, he acknowledged frankly that the union's resources wouldn't allow it to mount really effective widespread industrial action if that turned out to be necessary.

Everything now hinges on what Heath has to say in his Presidential-style televised Press conference which he is to give at Lancaster House tomorrow about Phase Two of his pay and prices policy. The newspapers have been well briefed in advance and it seems most unlikely that the civil servants will be allowed to catch up by the 20 per cent they now reckon to be behind other similar white-collar workers in outside industry. That is what they claim they were due to get from January 1st on the basis of the two-yearly 'fair comparisons' review of their salaries.

Any arbitrary wage freeze is bound to cause injustices and anomalies. Small ones might be swallowed but the pace of inflation in the past two years has left the Civil Service trailing badly – further behind than ever before. Hence the bitterness.

The most Bill Kendall and his colleagues expect from Heath is some sort of machinery to look at exceptional cases. But there is no real confidence that even that will be conceded.

After the rally I marched to Downing Street with the union and went with the senior officials to hand in a protest letter at No. 10. It was a rare and untypical display of militancy by these traditionally peaceful Government employees. But precisely how representative it was of grassroots feeling among civil servants throughout the country is less certain.

Industrial action by civil servants would be a grave development. The union needs to be very sure of the support it can command. But the Government would be foolish to dismiss the possibility lightly. Its actions on many issues since it took office have fuelled militancy and there are few groups of workers, white or blue-collared, who are now prepared to passively accept treatment they believe to be grossly unfair.

17th, Wednesday: This morning the 'Sun' ran an 800-words article by me setting out – 'boldly', according to the newspaper's editorial – why I favour a prices and incomes policy. The headline on my article was 'We must fight on Heath's ground.' I insisted we had to present our own viable and believable alternative policy on this crucial issue.

And I added: 'The unions know that Labour's search for credibility stretches far beyond Westminster and penetrates throughout their own ranks. It is not just the politicians who have to convince the public they mean what they say.'

The union leaders know this. The Party leaders know it. But nobody likes to say it openly. Everyone is afraid of upsetting someone else. Trades unionists need the Labour Party just as the Party needs the unions. Time is running out steadily and progress between the Party and the TUC has to be made on incomes policy to an extent that can be given some public presentation. Heath is slowly stealing more and more of Labour's clothes even though they are an uncomfortable fit.

I watched the Ted Heath Show on TV. The man is utterly uninspiring but it was done with confidence and competence.

But my initial reaction is that Phase Two will maintain too many injustices on pay, will not do anything like as much for the low-paid as Heath suggests and is inadequate on prices, dividends and profit margins. I rate industrial conflict almost inevitable unless there is a 'safety valve' tucked away in the small print of the White Paper to take care of those exceptional cases. I never much liked the phrase about 'dirty shabby compromises', coined by the former TUC general secretary George Woodcock, because compromises in these matters need not be dirty or shabby. What is certain is that they are essential in the broad sweep of industrial relations – just as they are in marital relations. This economic package seems to leave very little room for manoeuvre.

We are certain to have a lively Parliamentary session ahead. This issue will dominate it. Harold Wilson has been quoted on the radio as saying that we won't obstruct passage of the Bill in the House providing the Tories accept amendments. They have given nothing away in the form of amendments to major Bills in the past and I can't see them starting now.

It looks as though we shall be in the familiar 'No' Lobby when the votes come. There is political danger in going for total belligerent opposition. We have to avoid creating the impression that we are against any kind of incomes policy. That would make us appear to be indulging in exactly the same kind of acrobatics as we accused the Tories of. So we must plug away on the theme that it is the terms of this particular package which we can't swallow. We can give the Government a tough enough time that way. I took roughly this line when I spoke to my local Party management committee in Islington tonight. It proved to be acceptable although few of the delegates had really had time to digest the Government plans so discussion was inevitably inhibited.

18th, Thursday: This is the last week of the so-called Christmas recess. I seem to have spent most of it half-submerged in a sea of paper – letters, documents, leaflets, newspapers and periodicals. I have done far less reading than I had hoped would be possible, been out less with the family than intended and done virtually nothing around the house and garden. I am all in favour of a nine-day week.

Tonight I was at a County Hall meeting of the Labour Party's Regional Council publicity sub-committee. Tomorrow evening I have the surgery. That means every evening has been occupied this week. Next week I expect to be in the House every evening. That's politics.

19th, Friday: Often you work hard for a constituent and get no thanks at all. Occasionally you do very little and the gratitude is remarkable. I had a letter today from an immigrant constituent I helped over a student grant. He may well have got it without my intervention for all I know – but I felt like framing his letter to me!

It read:

'Your letter of 15th January, 1973, was received on 17th January. The contents the letter contained were joy-provoking ones.

'The happiest person on earth is somebody who dedicates himself to assist people who are in need of his help. I regard you as one of the persons in this very rare class. To be a leader is not an easy work. Time is always too short with many things to do.

'I came to the Party Rooms on 29th December, 1972. With many things to do, at a short possible time, you squeezed in the time we spent together to listen to all my complaints and took a very active action on it.

'This is indeed the art of leadership which is needed in every civilised country. For the first time I was not turned back disappointed. I came there with a heavy heart and from your letter I could see that the heavy heart is becoming lighter and lighter. In addition to this, it is now filled with JOY. The joy which will stabilise my concentration on my studies.

'Surely you have done what I will never forget and anywhere I may be in this life, I will never forget you. May the Lord Almighty be with you and your family and give you LONG LIFE to serve your beloved people for long. Once more, your kindness is appreciated.'

See what I mean about that frame.

There was a whole batch of housing cases at the 'surgery' tonight. Two of them are very difficult ones – both evictions.

The most urgent case was that of a family – husband, wife and year-old twin boys – who have to be out of their furnished accommodation by Tuesday when the bailiffs are due. The Greater London Council is apparently prepared to put them up in a dirty old tenement block without any means of heating. The husband told me he has chronic asthma, is unable to work and has been told by the doctor that he must have a warm home. He brought out about five or six different bottles of pills, each of which he has to take daily to keep going.

I can do nothing over the week-end but will chase up the Housing Department first thing Monday morning. I gave him a note to get him in to see the Housing Manager or one of her staff promptly after I have phoned her. But it will doubtless be complicated because the Islington and GLC Housing Departments are both involved and quite possibly the welfare services, too.

*   *   *

20th, Saturday: Today's constituency engagement brought no problems for a change. I went to the wedding reception for George Taylor, one of our councillars, who acted as my voluntary agent at the last General Election.

21st, Sunday: Harold Wilson's week-end speech in Edinburgh got plenty of attention in the Sunday newspapers. Perhaps some of them were still smarting somewhat from his bitter attack on the Press last week over its treatment of the Labour Party compared with its largely kid glove handling of the Tories.

But the importance of the speech was that it reflected an awareness of the necessity for the Party – and for its Leader in particular – to fight to retrieve the political initiative and try to forget all those internal squabbles. There was more than a mere touch of the pre-1964 Wilson about it; not so much in the theme which comprised an assault on the Tories for creating a remote and soulless society, together with some far-reaching policy pointers on, for instance, public ownership of the land, but in the overall impression it gave of a man and a Party able to recognise the mood and desires of the nation and to offer a positive response. True, there was rather more analysis of the problems than solutions to them. But then this was the first in a series of major speeches.

It could well be something of a turning point.

I watched Harold later in the late night TV discussion programme with Dick Crossman. He might be prepared to admit to rather more errors between 1964–70 than he does without damaging either himself or the Party. But Crossman's continual apologia for the bundle of mistakes made by a Government of which he was a very prominent member made me wonder how he ever stayed on in office while all around him was allegedly in disarray. I suppose Crossman has accumulated more wisdom with hindsight than any other contemporary politician. But it just could have something to do with the fact that he is not seeking re-election as a MP again and appears to want to establish himself as the most revealing and controversial historian of the 1970s.

Anyway, if Harold was a trifle complacent about the past, it's a change these days from the almost obsessional acts of contrition of some of his erstwhile Cabinet colleagues and overall this so-called non-political programme was a darned good Party Political Broadcast for us.

22nd, Monday: The House formally resumed today after the recess; but no votes were scheduled and MPs were thin on the ground. Things won't really get under way until tomorrow.

23rd, Tuesday: The Parliamentary Labour Party met specially this morning to decide on the Party's attitude towards the Government's latest counter-inflation measures, due to come before the House tomorrow.

There was some confusion among our MPs about just what line we would be adopting since Press reports of the Shadow Cabinet meeting last week were conflicting. But Harold Wilson nipped any doubts smartly in the bud by making it plain that we should be opposing the Government on the grounds that the overall package was unfair and unworkable – pretty much as expected.

He answered quite a few questions. The first came from assiduous Scots MP, Tam Dalyell who asked what Harold would say about Civil Service pay in his speech in tomorrow's debate. It was a point I had intended to raise myself had Tam not speedily done so. Harold was unequivocally firm in support of the civil servants and said that he would back them in his speech.

There was a mini-debate on the general situation with Tribune MPs Stan Orme and Eric Heffer airing again their known distaste for any kind of incomes policy in a mixed economy. Denis Healey, the Shadow Chancellor, didn't accept this view on incomes policy although he agreed with them that there is something of a crisis of capitalism building up. But he got a trifle extravagant when he suggested that Heath may have produced 'an arsenal for socialism'. True, we might be able to utilise some of the Tory proposals which, after all, smack of our own 1964–70 ideas in part. Denis was presumably thinking, in particular, of the machinery for price control. But his colourful and eminently reportable phrase was rather more vivid than justifiable.

Not everyone in the Party is entirely at ease over the all-out

opposition pose we are taking up. Fred Lee is a veteran engineering union MP and former Minister who has announced recently
that he won't seek to get back to the House at the next General
Election. Fred is a very genuine character and has generally
been regarded as Left of centre. But he has always proclaimed
himself in favour of a prices and incomes policy.

He was unable to get to the Party meeting. He was unhappy
when I told him what had happened. His fears were that we
might be thought to be against incomes policy in principle. I am
not sure that I was able to reassure him adequately on this
point.

The Chancellor, Anthony Barber, looked worried when I
quizzed him this afternoon about morale in the Customs and
Excise Department. I pointed out that, contrary to the impression
he gave in the House before Christmas, its morale was very un-
satisfactory. I had details of his meeting with staff side representatives recently and I said the difficulties arose mainly from
EEC entry, the implementation of VAT and 'the grossly unfair
treatment of the Civil Service in the current freeze'. I referred
to the heavy overworking involved. I asked: 'Isn't he setting the
worst possible example as an employer?' Barber parried and
claimed he had useful talks with the union people concerned.
But he knows that if these civil servants cut up rough over the
freeze just as VAT begins they could cause havoc.

The Bill to provide rent allowances for furnished tenants was
the main business of the Parliamentary day. Halfway through
the evening it looked as though we might run out of speakers.
Our Whips were searching around for Labour MPs to join the
debate. The Tories, of course, were quite content to get it over
early.

Our people thought we should be making more of it, even
though we are not opposing the measure. There are some considerable shortcomings. I was approached to speak but I reckoned
that if I did so, it would mar my chances of getting into tomorrow's debate on the Counter-Inflation Bill. So I opted out
and they managed to round up enough MPs to keep it going.
But it reflects rather badly on Parliament when this kind of
situation crops up and seems to me to call for a spot more
organisation in our own ranks. In fairness, there is an obvious
problem on the day after the recess. MPs who might have been

asked, in advance, to put in an appearance, have probably not been contactable.

24th, Wednesday: Several of last week-end's Sunday newspapers carried reports indicating that Phase 3 of the Government's counter-inflation policy, to follow the present measures we are to discuss, will be tougher still. There was a sharp reaction on the Stock Exchange on Monday with a big drop in share prices.

Heath was questioned about this by Harold Wilson at Question Time yesterday. Harold wanted to know if Heath accepted full responsibility for a Ministerial briefing last Saturday which led to the stories appearing. But Heath insisted that there was 'no such Ministerial action'.

So today I made some inquiries which confirmed that:

the briefing took place – but on Friday not Saturday;
it was given to Sunday newspaper industrial correspondents by Maurice Macmillan, the Employment Secretary;
he did suggest that Phase 3 would be tougher;
his interpretation conflicted with the line pushed by Heath at his own briefing held for certain Fleet Street editors earlier in the week.

I wrote a long note to Harold Wilson who was obviously anxious to get the fullest possible picture. I couldn't talk to him about it because he was already on the Front Bench listening to Heath opening the keynote debate on the counter-inflation proposals. He read my note and let me know that he wouldn't deal with the matter in his own speech. But he was ready if it cropped up and had also received other confirmation of what really happened.

Heath's speech was hardly greeted with enthusiasm by his own supporters on the Benches behind him. I intervened when he got to Civil Service pay to accuse him of discriminating against them. Inevitably, he denied this. But he spent a significant slice of this speech dealing with civil servants' pay and stressing that any anomalies could be looked at in Phase 3. It looks very much as though the arguing, lobbying and demonstrating by civil servants is having an effect.

Wilson was first-class. That was the generally accepted conclusion. Coming so soon after his Edinburgh speech, it means he has really regained much of the political initiative.

Our own Backbenchers, including those who frequently criticise him severely, lapped it up. And the Tories were silent apart from a testy intervention or two from Heath. They may well have had a request from their Whips to keep the temperature down and not to heckle. Whatever the reason they were glum as they saw Harold succeeding. One of the younger Tory MPs said to me later: 'He was certainly in top form.'

I had a chat with him later about the Macmillan briefing affair. He preferred to leave it to me to pursue rather than raise it himself and I will try to do so at Business Questions tomorrow by asking the Leader of the House, James Prior, to get the Prime Minister to make a personal statement.

Back in the Chamber, I checked with the Speaker, Selwyn Lloyd, and was told he hoped to be able to call me during the debate. I spoke for 13 minutes, attacking Heath for 'brazen hypocrisy' over his incomes policy switch, giving the whole package some stick, plugging away again at the civil servants' case and finally registering once again my support for a just prices and incomes policy.

Now I reckoned on having a bite to eat and a drink. I hadn't had time for either since lunchtime. But I got a 'green card' indicating that a constituent wanted to see me about civil servants' pay. I knew the Society of Civil Servants, which represents executive grades and is co-operating closely with the CPSA in the pay battle, was lobbying MPs tonight and that some CPSA members had joined in unofficially.

In the Lobby I met John Dryden, the Society's general secretary who asked me to go outside and speak to his members. There was a tremendous crocodile queuing up with placards and banners. I went up and down the line shouting out the latest position and ended up on a loud hailer which is not really permitted for speech-making in the precincts of the House. I was feeling pretty hoarse by the time I got back into the Chamber to hear the end of the debate. But the final speeches by Denis Healey and Barber proved to be rather an anticlimax.

*   *   *

25th, Thursday: I didn't get called at Business Questions after all. So I couldn't press on about the briefing. Instead, I sent a letter to Heath asking him to make a personal statement in the House. I released the letter for publication. That means the matter remains very much alive.

I kept two engagements outside the House. Firstly, at the BBC where I took part in a debate on the economy with Tory MP Barney Hayhoe, and then in Islington where I spent about an hour at a North London Teachers' Association function. I returned to the House for the voting at the end of the debate on the steel industry.

26th, Friday: The 'surgery' took more than 2½ hours tonight. As always, it was mostly housing. It all adds up to a lot of letter writing and probably telephoning on Monday morning.

29th, Monday: Tonight there was a meeting at the Commons of the Fabian Society's Trade Union Committee. The Society is a sort of socialist 'think-tank' with no collective policy. But it produces some valuable documents and last October published a tract called 'Towards a Radical Agenda' – its contribution to the debate on Labour's policy for the next General Election and beyond.

I was chairman of a working party which contributed an interim report on industrial relations to this particular document. It was a somewhat incomplete report and tonight's meeting discussed what to do about reviving the working party to carry on the job. Once again I was a bit inhibited. I have already decided I shall have to cut down on some of my commitments because of the new Front Bench role. I couldn't tell the meeting about this but I dropped a hint about difficulties ahead and I think I shall have to pack up the chairmanship although I shall stay on the working party to give it some continuity.

30th, Tuesday: Heath was off to Washington for his talks with Nixon but before he went I managed to ruffle his feathers again over the briefing issue.

I hadn't really made up my mind to try and raise it during Question Time but the choice was made for me by Harold Walker, our junior Front Bench spokesman on employment. He asked the Prime Minister to 'come clean' about the matter.

Heath said tersely that he had already explained the position very clearly to the House during debate – which he certainly hadn't. He said he sent a letter to me in reply to my letter which had been published and there was no reason why his shouldn't be. That seemed odd. Because I had released his reply when I received it. There was nothing confidential about it – and the morning papers had used it. *The Times*, which ran a major front-page story about the whole affair, printed the Heath letter in full. I wondered if he hadn't read his *Times*.

I stood up to have a say. Since the Prime Minister had referred to me, convention required the Speaker to call me. I said Heath was 'most evasive', both in reply to Harold Walker and to me in his letter. I again urged him to put the record straight but he complained that my remarks were 'absolutely unjustifiable'. He went on to claim that *The Times* report failed to support my allegations – an opinion which I don't share at all. At least his answer showed he did read *The Times*.

A number of our Members told me they thought he was on the run on this one. He knows he misled the House.

There have been some pretty glum faces on the Government Front Bench in the past few days. And for that matter the Back Bench Tories are miserable. As one of our older MPs said to me: 'It happened to us in Government. There was a period when everything seemed to start going wrong. However hard you tried, things seemed to backfire.'

31st, Wednesday: I wrote a carefully to-the-point letter to *The Times* today on the briefing affair and delivered it myself on my way to the House. I said Heath had played with words and turned his slogan about 'open government' into 'brief and deny'. I insisted he should admit he misled the Commons.

I got that GLC election address finally sorted out at lunchtime and on its way to the Greater London Labour Party. I am far happier with it than I was with the manifesto. It's due to go

D

through every letter-box so if we win I reckon I shall have a special reason to feel pleased.

This afternoon our Expenditure Committee sub-committee saw the National Union of Teachers about youth employment. But I cut my attendance short to go into the Chamber and take part in the debate on the Consolidated Fund (No. 2) Bill – a daunting title which conceals legislation approving certain extra funds for Government spending.

It gives Members a chance to have a series of mini-debates on anything they can fairly or sometimes imaginatively link to these Departmental estimates. Willie Hamilton had secured time to bring up the matter of pay for Department of Health and Social Security staff and hospital ancillary workers – the cleaners, cooks, gardeners and so on. The DHSS situation enables the whole Civil Service pay argument to come up again and I agreed to give Willie some support.

There were no Tories anxious to speak on this. Laurie Pavitt, Labour MP for West Willesden and a health service specialist, joined in on hospital pay, then I did six or seven minutes on civil servants. I warned the Government against using disciplinary measures if civil servants were involved in any form of industrial action. I said that could only escalate any dispute into 'a most grave confrontation'.

I had volunteered to serve on the Standing Committee (the name for committees dealing with Bills) on the Counter-inflation proposals. I learned I was to be one of the eighteen Labour members. So there is a hard slog ahead. But it should be quite an historic Committee to be in on.

February

1st, Thursday: This morning the Labour MPs making up the
Counter-inflation Bill team met to decide our strategy and dis-
cuss the amendments we are tabling to the Tory proposals. Reg
Prentice and Tony Benn will lead for us.

We had some lively argument but there was general agreement eventually that our approach should be one of 'controlled
militancy', although there may well be varied interpretations of
that as the Committee stage progresses. If we filibuster though
the Tories will introduce a guillotine, meaning they can fix a
timetable to suit themselves. They will then accused us of trying to delay the Bill. That would not normally be anything to
worry about, but with this Bill it would mean the pay freeze stays
on and some groups of workers, like the farmworkers who cannot
have their due rises until this Bill becomes an Act, would hardly
thank us for procrastination.

It is obvious that we shall have some widely differing views
expressed from our side about future pay policy, particularly
under a Labour Government. Tribune MP Stan Orme, for instance, is a member of the Committee and will doubtless knock
any kind of incomes policy in a mixed economy; but several
other Tribune MPs at the meeting took a different line from Stan.

Anyway our differences are unlikely to be as sharp as those on
the Tory side. 'Rebel' MPs Nicholas Ridley, who was sacked by
Heath from a Ministerial post, and Powellite John Biffen are on
the Committee and could well cause the Government some
trouble, most probably on the matter of the Prices and Pay
Commission having powers to take decisions which Parliament
is unable to question.

I had my question about Howard Hughes answered in the
Chamber today. But time has killed any interest in this. Home

Office Parliamentary Under Secretary David Lane denied any preferential treatment for Hughes when he arrived at Gatwick Airport and although I scoffed at that, it's a dead duck now.

Tonight I was told that my Front Bench appointment would at last be announced tomorrow along with some other changes.

I had a chat with Gregor Mackenzie, the Shadow Posts and Telecommunications Minister, to sort out roughly our 'demarcation' lines. He has been dealing with broadcasting and will continue to look after the technical aspects, directly related to the Post Office. I shall cover all other broadcasting matters, including the currently controversial area of programme content, highlighted by the Independent Broadcasting Authority's problems over the temporary High Court ban on showing the TV film about the offbeat film-maker and artist Andy Warhol. There is also the row that has blown up because the IBA itself has stopped the showing of a Granada film about Poulson, the consultant whose bankruptcy proceedings have dragged in the names of all sorts of prominent public figures, often in a thoroughly unjustified way.

There are questions to Sir John Eden, the Minister of Posts and Telecommunications, next Wednesday and I shall be sharing the Opposition Front Bench responsibility for dealing with them with Gregor Mackenzie.

2nd, Friday: Willie Hamilton's Bill to outlaw discrimination against women failed to get a Second Reading this afternoon. It was a technicality that ditched it and prevented it going to a Committee – the second time this has happened. There was uproar from our side of the House but the Speaker seemed to have no option other than to rule that it couldn't go ahead. The decision was unpalatable to the vast majority of MPs crowding the Chamber. Most of us turned up specially to try and ensure it progressed if there was a vote on it. But the Speaker said it had not had the required two hours debate by 4 o'clock and that was that. It was a farcical situation and the Women's Lib battalion in the public gallery vented their understandable feelings.

3rd, Saturday: The morning newspapers mostly gave a reasonable mention to my new job. The *Guardian* called the appointment 'intriguing'.

But there was 'no blood on it' unlike the omission from the Front Bench team of Tribune MP Eric Heffer as one of Reg Prentice's two deputies on employment. Eric Heffer released his letter to Harold Wilson, complaining that Reg didn't take a tough enough line in fighting the Tories on industrial relations, that he had attacked the dockers who were sent to prison for defying the Industrial Relations Act and that he simply couldn't work with him. This parting of the ways has been inevitable for some time. Eric had threatened resignation before and Reg had let it be known that he had no regrets. I doubt if it will cause much excitement inside the PLP since everyone has been expecting it. But, looked at from the political journalists' viewpoint, it was the best angle in the story about the new Front Bench line-up. And Friday's not usually much of a day for political news.

5th, Monday: We got under way on the Counter-Inflation Bill at 4 o'clock this afternoon. It looks very much as though Maurice Macmillan, the Secretary of State for Employment who is leading the Government team, is in for a sticky time. Still he has a couple of smooth operators with him on the Tory Front Bench to help him through – Patrick Jenkin, Chief Secretary to the Treasury which is the No. 2 job to the Chancellor, and Kenneth Baker, Parliamentary Secretary for the Civil Service.

There are twenty-one Tories and one Liberal, along with our eighteen members, making up the Committee. If Ridley, Biffen and John Pardoe, the Liberal, do vote with us, the Government loses. But if part of the Bill is thrown out in Committee, the Government can seek to restore it when it goes back to the whole House of Commons for its 'report' stage debate. Even so, defeat on anything of consequence in Committee would be a highly embarrassing setback for Macmillan.

Because of the importance of the issue this is an unusually large Committee and is using Room 10, the biggest of the first floor committee rooms. The chairman is Labour MP Carol Johnson who has to adopt a strictly impartial role throughout. He is drawn from a panel of senior MPs who, irrespective of Party, chair all these Standing Committees – as the committees dealing with Bills are called.

He sits under a huge painting entitled 'Alfred inciting the

Saxons to prevent the landing of the Danes'. The Government supporters sit in the seats on his right and the Opposition on his left, just as they sit on either side of the Speaker in the Chamber.

The public are able to attend these Standing Committees but many people just don't realise it. It's a pity really because they often provide better genuine debate than you get in the Chamber. The essential difference is that anyone can seek to speak at any point of the proceedings and as often as they like. The chairman doesn't close the debate until all those wanting to talk have done so. It lends itself to filibustering but that's not a really common occurrence.

We started with Reg Prentice accepting the Government's 'sittings' motion that the Committee should meet on Monday and Tuesday afternoons and for virtually all day on Thursdays. He pointed out that these were abnormally long hours for a committee – Members have to fit in all their usual activities, too – and said they would compress into a little over a fortnight the equivalent of what would otherwise be done in about nine weeks if committee sittings were spread over as normal on Tuesday and Thursday mornings. He explained that despite our hostility to the Bill, we recognised that delaying it only meant the freeze stayed in force.

Nevertheless, Stan Orme felt obliged to register his protest against any indication that we were acquiescing to a speedy passage of the Bill.

We moved on to a request to the Chairman to tell us about dinner break times and to arrange to have our voting divisions flashed up on the TV annunciators dotted around the House. Customarily, these announcements are only screened for the annual Standing Committee on the Finance Bill. But both Government and Opposition agreed that this Committee deserved similar treatment. It means Members will be able to stray a little further from the Committee room without fear of missing a vote. Carol Johnson said he would allow $1\frac{1}{4}$ hours each evening for dinner.

Then we got into a fair old row about how we could deal properly with the Bill and the pay and prices boards it sets up without getting from Macmillan the Code of Practice under which they will operate. We complained bitterly because the Code will eventually go to the House in a form that will not allow amendments. It will be a straight vote on the lot and that means, in effect, that the Government will have its way without even a comma altered.

Macmillan refused to come clean on when the House would get the Code. There was a deal of pressure on this point and I said that if it was available to our Committee it would alter our time-table – but I suspected he had no intention of producing it while we were sitting and should say so. The carping paid off. He reluctantly admitted it was unlikely we would get it before the Committee ended its work.

After some further procedural wrangling, we settled down to consider the clauses dealing with the establishment of the pay and prices agencies. The Labour theme was the unfair, unworkable and undemocratic nature of the whole package. Throughout the evening the missing Code figured prominently in the speeches. But by 11.50 p.m. when we packed up for the night, we were none the wiser about its contents.

6th, Tuesday: I let Walter Harrison, our Deputy Chief Whip, know that I want to quit the Expenditure Committee. It's the kind of involvement that takes up quite a lot of time if you do the job properly and I really need that time now. It's regarded as something of a 'plum' committee so Walter won't have trouble filling my spot.

We had fun and games in the Standing Committee. It was all a bit of a 'red herring' really. Maybe a pink one. It arose from a story in the pink-paged *Financial Times* this morning. The newspaper's lobby correspondent, John Bourne, an old friend of mine from our days as industrial correspondents, had his own version of the Code splashed all over Page One.

Macmillan stumbled around and we spent two hours haranguing him, forcing him to admit that working documents existed, that he knew more than he would tell and so on.

Unlike the Gallery writers, who report on what's said on the Floor of the House, the lobby men interpret the political news. I rate this story less of a 'leak' than a piece of intelligent, well-informed interpretation. There was no quote from any document or precise mention of one, other than the already-published White Paper on the proposals.

My colleagues asked me where I reckoned the story came from. I said people are inevitably wrong when they speculate about journalists' sources. But if I had to guess, I would think that either a knowledgeable Minister or civil servant had given John Bourne a fair insight into how the Government was thinking about certain key aspects. Add in a dash of common sense, top it up with background from the White Paper and there's your recipe. But the unfortunate Macmillan found it all very difficult to explain away.

7th, Wednesday: Today was my D for Début day on the Front Bench for questions to the Posts and Telecommunications Minister, Sir John Eden. I had run through the Order Paper in advance with Gregor Mackenzie so that there was no 'who does what' problem.

It's not very usual for a Front Bench spokesman to put down questions on his own subject, although it's done from time to time, but I had one tabled prior to my appointment. It concerned IBA programme content and was really aimed at the Warhol case.

I was pretty nervous, though nothing like as bad as when I asked my first-ever Parliamentary question from the Back Bench or when I made my 'maiden' speech. Many Members on our side have been trade union officers, teachers, lawyers or maybe just had the advantage of university debating club membership. They prattle away quite merrily without a note – though I must say that those who fail to prepare their remarks seldom come off. Powell, for instance, rarely has a note in evidence but spends hours in the Commons Library, brooding over his homework. It pays.

But my job for years was listening and writing, not speaking. I suppose it's coming gradually, though.

As for the nerves, some very experienced Members have told me they still suffer terribly if they are due to speak, particularly from the Despatch Box.

I had tried to prepare some replies on several questions where it seemed I should intervene. But they didn't turn out to be appropriate. Anyway I said my little piece concerning the Warhol case and Eden gave me the customary courteous welcome to the

Front Bench before replying. It was hardly a striking first appearance but at least I didn't put my foot in it.

Later I had a brief chat with Harold Wilson to clear up one or two points about the job and sent a letter, explaining my role, to the lobby correspondents' secretary since quite a few of them had been asking me just what the appointment means.

8th, Thursday: I scored a small personal victory in the Standing Committee this morning. I attacked the Bill's proposal that evidence to the pay and price agencies should be taken in secret on request. Any witness could claim this right and the chairmen of the agencies hadn't even discretionary power to turn it down. I said the unions wouldn't want secrecy over their demands. It simply protected the price-fixers who need give no excuse at all in ensuring the public was excluded.

Patrick Jenkin stonewalled. He consulted his Treasury advisers and said there were precedents. I retorted that it was deplorable and we had already agreed that the legislation in this case was unprecedented. I kept going and Reg Prentice came in to back me. Finally, Jenkin had words with Macmillan and said he thought there was a good deal in what I said. The Government would reconsider.

Another slight ordeal later. I had tabled a question to Heath a couple of weeks earlier, asking him to make a statement about the Franks Committee recommendations for reform of the Official Secrets Act. Now I was entitled to ask about this from the Front Bench. Indeed, it is the kind of issue I must be involved with.

A negative reply was inevitable. I came back with what I thought was quite a sharp supplementary question, accusing the Prime Minister of hedging on his promise of open government to which, I suggested, the *Financial Times* was currently contributing more than he was.

Heath, who I am happy to observe, doesn't seem to like me one bit, was a bit needled and gave a testy answer. I thought our own Backbenchers might have rumbled a bit at him. But in the tearoom later Jimmy Dunn, one of our Whips, told me I couldn't be heard properly from the back of the Chamber because I had stood between two sets of microphones – a tip to remember.

The Standing Committee resumed this afternoon. There was a prolonged and often quite philosophical debate on price controls. It was 12.20 a.m. when we got away.

9th, Friday: An elderly couple came to see me at the 'surgery' as 'our last resort'. They have been on the housing waiting list for 27 years. Their home is damp, heated only by paraffin heaters and lacks hot water. It isn't self-contained and eight people use the single toilet at the house. They admitted that a lot of people in the area live in worse conditions than they do. But after all that time, they asked, couldn't they get a small one-bedroomed flat with their own front door to close behind them? It doesn't seem much to ask.

But there are so many in the queue, trapped like this, that I know it would be wrong to send them away with high hopes. Once again I can only say I'll try. And I'm not optimistic.

I called briefly on a satisfied 'customer' on the way home – an American who I had recently helped to overcome delay in getting naturalisation papers from the Home Office. He was celebrating with a party for friends and neighbours and was grateful enough to invite me along.

12th, Monday: It was a particularly lively day for me on the Standing Committee. We were on to pay and I had some pungent and newsworthy points to make about the Civil Service claim. Bill Kendall, the CPSA general secretary, and a couple of his colleagues came along to listen.

Reg Prentice opened the debate by firmly dissociating himself from anyone seeking organised industrial confrontation between the unions and the Government over the policy. But he went on to warn of the anger and militancy the Government has caused.

I was called next. I began with some general remarks about pay, said a little about the claims of the gas workers, the farm-workers and the London teachers and argued that 'moderates have been turned into militants and militants into martyrs'.

I moved on to the Civil Service situation which I dealt with in some detail. Then I brought the matter right home to the Committee. I said the CPSA's Houses of Parliament branch has offered majority support for the union's one-day strike. I explained that a special agreement between the House authorities and the union accepted 'the absolute necessity that the work of ... Commons must not be impeded'. I said that it appeared that if the union officially encouraged the strike, the general secretary could be impeached, called before the Bar of the House and imprisoned as a result of any disruption.

I drew attention to Bill, sitting in the public seats, waiting to know what terrible fate might await him. The Parliamentary reporters were quickly on to this and Bill gave an impromptu Press conference outside the room. It guaranteed good Press coverage for the union case next day although we were not at all sure that the branch would ultimately want to go ahead. Even so, it was a good illustration of the resentment felt.

The pay debate went on after the dinner break and I decided to have another go. I raised the week-end leading articles in *The Times* and the *Sunday Telegraph*. These newspapers, ostensibly uncompromising supporters of the Government's pay policy, had referred to a pay dispute in Fleet Street last week. It was eventually settled by the Newspaper Publishers' Association, the employers' 'union', on the terms of the clerical workers who went on strike.

The Times pontificated that as a member of the NPA it was bound by the agreement but 'as an individual newspaper it is the consistent policy of *The Times* Executive not to give way to this sort of pressure'. It added that 'we should be humbugs to pretend that the NPA seems to us to have set the right example'.

I suggested that the humbug went right through that editorial and asked: 'Why doesn't *The Times* tear up its existing agreement with the NPA? I am not arguing that that would necessarily be a good or bad thing but how can this newspaper accuse the NPA of impropriety and, at the same time, remain happily in membership? In this matter of what it considers to be of supreme national importance why is it toeing the NPA line?'

I had a smack at the *Sunday Telegraph* for expressing similar views and asked Macmillan for his opinion of the facing-both-ways attitude of his Fleet Street allies. When he ultimately replied to the debate Macmillan said he was having the newspaper deal looked into and – responding to my further questioning – he said if there had been an infringement of the standstill he could act upon it.

I had had a couple of highly satisfactory innings. It was 12.20 a.m. when I left for home.

13th, Tuesday: If I hadn't been on the Standing Committee it would have been a splendid week to catch up on much of my outstanding 'homework' relating to the Front Bench job. There are hardly any Whipped votes. As it is, I am tied to Committee Room 10.

Still, it's proving an interesting assignment and often quite a stimulating one. The Government suffered its first defeat in the Committee today. Ridley and Biffen voted for an amendment to the Bill which means the Government's powers under it must be renewed annually by Parliament instead of every three years – the Government proposal. Macmillan blundered by making the vote a major test of Government credibility rather than playing the whole thing down, ready to restore his own plan at 'report' stage of the Bill when the whole House votes on it.

His tactless speech ensures that the Press will report the defeat as a major embarrassment for the Government. The House adjourned soon after 8 p.m. this evening but the Committee ploughed on. The Tories were worried about their timetable and insisted on pushing ahead to reach Clause 8 of the Bill before we packed up.

It meant we sat on into the night, tired, disinclined to probe really adequately and prolong the session even more and as Neil Kinnock, Bedwellty's redhaired Labour Member, said to me: 'It's a bloody silly way to run a country.' So it is. It was well after 2 a.m. when we finished.

14th, Wednesday: Neither *The Times* nor *Daily Telegraph* carried a line about my abrasive references to them in the Standing Committee despite the fact that I let their Parliamentary staff know in advance of my intentions. It is hard to see it as anything other than suppression.

I shouldn't have bothered any more if they had used a paragraph or two. As it is, I began gathering signatures for a Com-

mons motion rapping both newspapers. I shall table it tomorrow
and it will be difficult for them to ignore it again once it is on
the Order Paper.

The Standing Committee has kept me so busy that I have
largely lost track of events on the Floor of the House. But Willie
Hamilton's Anti-Discrimination Bill came back to the Commons
tonight. Women's Lib and other supporters of this overdue
measure packed the gallery again and despite some speeches
against it those Tory backwoodsmen didn't have the courage to
force a division this time. So a Second Reading was approved
without a vote and the Bill goes to a Committee for consideration. Better late than never.

15th, Thursday: Heath was stupidly childish at Question Time
over the gas workers dispute. He accused Reg Prentice of being
irresponsible for supporting a call for a court of inquiry. That's
the last thing anyone can fairly call Reg in his handling of industrial relations.

There is a growing anxiety on our side and quite a bit of tearoom talk about the extent to which Heath is seeking a showdown. The gas workers' decision to take industrial action over
their pay demand could provide him with a General Election
platform of 'Who governs – the Government or the unions?' It
sounds attractive for the Tories on the face of it. But it's an
immense risk for them to take. They have a workable Parliamentary majority and could soldier on for another couple of
years.

A General Election could give them an increased majority and
a superficial mandate to deal with the unions even more
stringently – or try to. What it would, in fact, produce if they
fought on those narrow lines would be a country more bitterly
divided than ever, given a Tory victory.

Labour though, wouldn't allow the battle theme to be confined in such a way. The Common Market, food prices, rents,
housing and land prices, pensions and a host of other issues
would all be chucked in by us.

Heath's no gambling man. He won't go to the country unless
he either has to or is very sure of his chances. He is not yet in
either situation.

There is one other possibility which could induce him to act in the next few months – one which I have long considered the most likely reason for a Spring 1973 poll. Prices remain out of control. VAT will add to the trouble. The initial costs of Market entry will begin to show – and that old balance of payments enemy is looking dangerous all over again as the surplus he inherited from Labour is frittered away. Things will get a lot worse for him before they get better and the temptation must be there.

Our Standing Committee met for most of the day. I had a brush with Dame Pat Hornsby-Smith, the Chislehurst Tory MP, over the lousy council house building record of Bromley – the borough which contains her seat. I was a Party activist there for a long time and I bashed Bromley for failing to help solve the housing problems of inner London. We had a couple of brisk exchanges in which she defended her local Tories in the face of a pretty lamentable record.

16th, Friday: There was a tricky advice bureau case tonight involving a complaint against the police. The woman concerned, whose husband was in trouble and has a police record, complained that she had been taken to the police station, stripped and searched, all on unjustified suspicion of theft. I shall take up the matter with the Divisional Commander and will doubtless get another side of the story.

Whatever he says I doubt if I will even secure an apology for her if there is any belief that she might seek formal redress for wrongful arrest. An apology would be tantamount to an advance admission that a mistake had been made.

17th, Saturday: The Party's Greater London Region annual conference met at Camden Town Hall. I was one of the platform array as an executive member.

Harold Wilson was the guest speaker to give an extra push to our GLC election campaign. He was a shade too long. But he got in some good cracks at Heath's expense, some timely praise for our GLC manifesto and a good lambasting of Heath for his handling of the gathering pay crisis in which the gas workers and

civil servants now look sure to be followed in widespread industrial action by car workers, hospital workers and locomen.

These conferences rarely inspire anyone and this one seemed
unlikely to be any exception despite the forthcoming election
fight. The delegates ploughed through untidy debates on education and employment. The liveliest argument came over an
emergency motion from the Young Socialists calling on the TUC
to hold a twenty-four hour General Strike in support of the gas
workers. But the executive was not anxious to tell the TUC its
business. The trade union members were especially averse to
doing so. And the motion was soundly defeated.

The executive election results were announced at the end of
the day's session. I was joint top in the poll for four representatives for my area but there were one or two casualties, including Ashley Bramall, the Inner London Education Authority
Leader. It looked like a slight swing to the Left.

18th, Sunday: We could have tossed away the GLC election at
the regional conference today. A lengthy and utterly unrealistic
motion from the Young Socialists demanded changes in the
manifesto to include scrapping the rent rises imposed under the
Tory Housing Finance Act and also called on our GLC candidates
to pledge themselves to this or quit.

Leading figures like Reg Goodwin and Ashley Bramall had
previously made it clear that they couldn't fight on that kind of
programme. Many of the candidates had been picked by their
constituency parties in full knowledge that they would not back
a policy of non-implementation. And every Labour-controlled
London borough has now reluctantly agreed to operate the Act.

If the motion had gone through there would have been an
incredible crisis. It would have meant not just the reselection of
candidates but abandonment of the published manifesto and quite
a deal of other printed election material. Some constituency
parties would doubtless have gone ahead with the candidates
already selected anyway since the conference has no overriding
authority to instruct them on who to pick.

It all sounds too barmy to contemplate. It would have been a
gift to GLC Tory Leader Sir Desmond Plummer. They could
have got the red carpet out for him right away at County Hall.

Yet there was substantial support for the proposal from the floor of the conference. The executive opposed it, of course. Ron Pepper, a Lewisham councillor and comprehensive school head-master, put the platform case most effectively. He had originally proposed non-implementation of the Act in his own borough council so his credentials were pretty good; he had been in the front line and he won the argument hands down. But he was booed and heckled for all that. Eventually the delegates rejected the motion by a majority of around 2 to 1. Sanity prevailed.

19th, Monday: Posts and Telecommunications' questions have been shifted from Wednesdays to Mondays for reply and that put me back in business again on the Front Bench.

Any time now the Minister, Sir John Eden, is expected to announce that there is to be no wide-ranging inquiry into broad-casting, that the BBC and ITA should carry on as they are but that the fourth channel is quite possibly to go to ITV2 – com-mercial TV. I wanted to pre-empt that statement and after con-sultation with Harold Wilson I was able to declare to the House for the Opposition that if the Government took this course an incoming Labour Government would not feel bound by the de-cision and would reconsider the whole position.

As the questions went on there was a hubbub in the public gallery and several shouting Welsh language demonstrators were ejected. I made another brief intervention from the Despatch Box and referred, in passing, to the gallery incident. There were some shouts which sounded like 'Order' from the Tory Benches which didn't really register at all with me until I sat down and was reminded that you aren't supposed to acknowledge anything that happens in the gallery.

I recalled the gas bomb incident when the Chamber had to be evacuated in great haste. Hansard, the official report of the proceedings, merely recorded that moment of high drama as an interruption. It's another of those idiotic conventions which MPs seem quite happy to preserve.

Upstairs in the Standing Committee, we were moving towards the close. We finished at 12.30 a.m. and the whole Committee stage now looks sure to wrap up within 24 hours – just about in line with the Government's original timetable.

20th, Tuesday: Harold Wilson threw out an interesting proposal at Prime Minister's Question Time. He suggested Royal Commission powers for the new Government Pay Board to enable it to produce a more rapid report on the gas dispute. It may not be the perfect solution but Heath is over a barrel. Outright rejection would seem like deliberate warmongering. Yet acceptance would entail Harold getting credit for peacemaking and it seems certain that the idea would not have been advanced without some sounding being taken from the leadership of the General and Municipal Workers' Union, the principal union involved. Heath trod carefully and said he would fully consider.

I had something to say about inflationary rate rises during the Standing Committee session. Later on, I tried to tempt Maurice Macmillan into commenting on the Wilson peace proposal but he refused to be drawn.

The Committee finally wound up around 1.0 a.m. to everyone's obvious relief. It had, however, been a worthwhile operation on our side. Our team had all contributed effectively, with no passengers apparent. And we had achieved widespread publicity for our constant attacks on the Government – attacks which were regularly underscored by those two Tory 'rebels' who helped us maintain Press interest to the last. Now the Government has a repair job to do on the Bill before its Report Stage on the Floor of the House next week. The Government will no doubt have its way when MPs vote in their entirety – but not without further embarrassment.

21st, Wednesday: Along with three other Labour MPs, I lunched with some of the BBC 'top brass' at the West London TV Centre.

Back at the House the main debate was on an Opposition motion calling for free TV licences for pensioners. Our Social Services spokesman, John Silkin, opened skilfully although one of our own Backbenchers accused the Opposition of hypocrisy for demanding now what it failed to do in office. That was a gift to the Tories. Gregor Mackenzie supplied a spirited winding-up speech but Sir Keith Joseph, the Social Services Minister, scoffed at the whole idea and although several Tories abstained we lost the vote.

One small bright spot. I have managed to acquire a new office in Star Chamber Court, part of the Parliamentary building which is fairly accessible to the Chamber. True, I'm about four floors up and the lift doesn't go that high. But it's near enough to the centre of activity to make it worth using unlike my former berth.

22nd, Tuesday: There was a pretty violent clash at Question Time between Heath and Harold Wilson. Heath, replying to the Wilson proposal to give Royal Commission powers to the Pay Board, was told by the Opposition Leader that he was 'flatly rejecting' the scheme and 'must now bear the full responsibility for industrial disruption which follows'.

Heath retorted that this view was 'absolutely, completely and utterly mistaken'. He said the Pay Board would be set up urgently and Maurice Macmillan would meet the unions tomorrow. But it doesn't really look as though there is any intention to compromise and that can only spell prolonged trouble.

Heath was on TV tonight. It seems to me that the public relations men have been working overtime on him to stop him appearing abrasive, arrogant and haughty-sounding when he appears on 'the box'.

They can't get rid of that plummy voice but he kept it all very cool and was almost jocular in admitting he has given his housekeeper more weekly cash for the shopping. He went on to blithely pretend that his relations with the unions remain good despite the differences. This is arrant nonsense but some folk may be taken in a bit by his newfound air of sweet reasonableness.

23rd, Friday: I was in the House prepared to vote for a Private Member's Bill which sought to establish independent review tribunals to deal with complaints by or about the police. Its sponsor was Labour MP Philip Whitehead.

I am generally in favour of independent review bodies and have long thought something on these lines for the police to be necessary. So, it seems, does Robert Carr, the Home Secretary. He announced an independent ombudsmen to head a review body which he expected to start work before the end of the year. Philip Whitehead sensibly withdrew his Bill and no vote was needed.

It was quite a lengthy 'surgery' tonight – mostly housing cases, as usual. There was also a Mauritian whose nephew has been refused a visa to enter Britain after paying £260 to a computer training school which led him to believe he would be sure to be allowed in to take their course. It looks as though the fee he paid will be non-returnable – yet another swindle. I shall pursue this matter with the Home Office and take the opportunity of reminding them that it is about time they replied to the overall case I have made out to them in this whole shabby affair of these schools.

27th, Tuesday: Sixteen Labour MPs and a couple of Labour peers were at ATV's Marble Arch headquarters this morning to view a film, 'Hang Out Your Brightest Colours' – the life story of Michael Collins, the Irish rebel leader. It is the work of actor-producer Kenneth Griffiths but has been banned for showing by ATV chief Sir Lew Grade for whom Griffiths had made the film.

I arranged the showing with Grade after approaches from a number of interested Labour MPs who found the ban worrying and also after talking to Griffiths who was most anxious that we should have an opportunity to see it for ourselves.

Was it political censorship? Grade assured me that it was his decision and his alone – although the Independent Broadcasting Authority had seen the film. Grade is an impresario and hardly qualified to make a political judgment but he nevertheless was adamant that this film could prove explosive in the potent situation prevailing in Ulster today.

Surprisingly, quite a few of the Labour MPs who saw it ended up by agreeing with him. There was no consensus view, even though no showing was planned for Northern Ireland anyway. Certainly, Griffiths makes no attempt throughout the course of this disturbingly brilliant production to hide his impassioned belief that British imperialism is the real historical culprit in Ireland and that Lloyd George and Churchill, in particular, were rogues just as Collins was a hero.

It went far beyond the realms of documentary without, so far as I am aware, being inaccurate in any way factually. I could appreciate Grade's anxieties. Yet, on balance, I feel it should be shown. I think it highly improbable that it would have the dire consequences Grade considers possible. And it might do something to help create a better understanding this side of the Irish sea of the seemingly insoluble Irish problem. It's one man's prejudiced view of history – but, as I told Griffiths, that's no criticism. History, like beauty, is almost inevitably in the eye of the beholder.

Back at the House I found I was in demand. Journalists wanted my comments on the film. It was also the day of the civil servants' one-day protest strike over their pay. Union head office wanted to talk to me and the BBC wanted me to broadcast on the strike issue.

Heath had another stormy Question Time mainly over a weekend speech by Willie Whitelaw, the Secretary of State for Northern Ireland, which crudely and tactlessly sought to equate current industrial action by trades unionists against the Government pay policy with terrorist tactics in Ulster. It was a disgusting outburst and destroyed much of the enhanced reputation Whitelaw had built up in the House since he went to his unenviable post.

The kindest comment I heard was that Whitelaw, MP for Penrith and the Borders, was upset because he had watched Arsenal knock Carlisle out of the FA Cup on Saturday. More seriously, I have always rated the man inept when he gets on to the serious bread and butter domestic issues of politics. He proved this with past performances when he was Leader of the House – not when dealing with Parliamentary business matters but when called on to wind up certain important debates for the Government.

28th, Wednesday: I spent an hour at lunchtime with the 'Over 50s' Club in the Highbury area of my constituency, talking to them about my work as a MP and answering their very lively questions. I should have been back at the House by at least 3.30 p.m. when we were due to begin the second and final day of the Report stage of that Counter-Inflation Bill. We could have votes at any time. I was pretty sure there would be no immediate vote, however, and it was just as well that I was right about that. It was the day of the locomen's strike and the traffic was jammed most of the way from Islington to Westminster. The 15 minutes journey took me 50 minutes and I was 20 minutes late getting to the House.

Today saw the publication of a joint Labour Party-TUC statement of aims for the next Labour Government. This seems to be an important breakthrough to what Harold Wilson and Vic Feather are both saying should be a 'great compact'. There will inevitably be sharp criticism that it doesn't spell out just what the unions can deliver on pay but despite that gap it should help to convince the public that Labour can achieve the kind of essential working relationship with the unions that must underpin our economic prosperity and can never be gained under the Tories. Tory Central Office was sufficiently worried about it to rush out a statement by their Party chairman, Lord Carrington, branding the Labour Party-TUC plans as a sellout to militants.

Much of the discussion in the House centred on tomorrow's by-elections at Lincoln, Chester-le-Street and Dundee. Special circumstances surround all three and must blur their longterm significance. Taverne, the pro-Market former Labour MP, is running on his independent Labour ticket against John Dilks, our official candidate. Chester-le-Street, rock solid Labour by tradition, could nonetheless be affected by the backwash of the Poulson bankruptcy proceedings during which various leading lights in the Labour Party in the North-east have been referred to. And Dundee's MP was another pro-Market man, George Thomson, who quit to take up his top EEC job in Brussels.

It looks as though quite a few voters will boycott the two major parties in a 'plague on both your houses' spirit. And the rumour is that tomorrow's newspaper opinion polls will show a big lead for Taverne at Lincoln.

If that attitude is restricted to by-elections it is not really very alarming. If it spread to a General Election it could have serious implications for democracy in Britain. The Liberals, in particular, might gain through their parish pump approach. It can sound attractive when peddled by a minority part which can afford to be glib and irresponsible because it has no prospect of power. But if the Liberals picked up many seats they would have to adopt coherent and responsible policies or our whole political currency would be devalued.

March

1st, Thursday: The newspaper opinion polls did indeed show
Taverne way ahead at Lincoln. He appears unstoppable but it
won't be the watershed in British politics that some pundits
continue to suggest.

I do not believe the result will teach us much we don't know
already – that people consider that governments of the Left and
Right have failed to fulfil their hopes in the past decade or
so and they will carry on using by-elections to demonstrate
their disenchantment. Where we must react is in the formula-
tion and presentation of our future policy. This has been
recognised and was reflected in last year's document, 'Labour's
Programme for Britain,' which was approved by the Party
conference. That has to be sharpened up and updated as
the basis of a manifesto which states certain firm commitments
but avoids any pretence that Labour can provide a rapid cure-
all.

We should not lead people to believe that old favourites
like cuts in defence spending, scrapping Tory tax changes
and adding a wealth tax, will be enough to pay for the many
sweeping changes needed to combat poverty. Income redistribution cannot simply stop at the rich or await economic
growth. There are plenty of folk comfortably enough off to
make a somewhat larger cash contribution to help achieve
our aims and quite a few of them would accept the situation if the whys and wherefores were properly spelled out to
them.

If we really do mean to look after the old, the sick, the
handicapped and the jobless, to clean up slum housing and
schools and to raise our stake in the struggle against world
proverty, we can't hope to do it all by stealth.

2nd, Friday: Taverne cakewalked it at Lincoln with a 13,000 majority. But we clung on to Dundee and Chester-le-Street. Fortunately there was no comfort for the Tories – third in each race.

I was sorry to read in the newspapers of the resignation of Walter Anderson as general secretary of the National and Local Government Officers' Association, the world's biggest white-collared union. 'Andy' and his wife are old friends. He is regarded as one of the leading moderates on the TUC General Council. He believes the TUC should continue to talk to the Government about its pay policy and he opposes a boycott of the new Pay Board. But his own NALGO executive has decided to back the TUC line and he says he is 'not prepared to be a cypher'. He might well be regarded as an unwitting casualty of the Government's stupid anti-union policies which have edged white-collared unions like NALGO into adopting uncharacteristic militant postures.

5th, Monday: The TUC's special Congress overwhelmingly backed a proposal for a one-day general strike although unions are only 'invited' to join in. I sat in the gallery at Central Hall, Westminster, to watch what turned out to be the most muddled Congress I have attended and I have only missed one over the past 12 to 13 years. They are usually run extremely smoothly – far more so than Labour Party conferences. But this one got into all sorts of procedural tangles from the outset.

The TUC's report to the Congress failed to spell out any form of action to further its opposition to the Government. You didn't need a Congress to approve the economic strategy outlined in the document, but if you bring a big bunch of delegates to London after priming them with plenty of fiery oratory over a prolonged period, some of them already involved in strikes in their own industries, they are bound to want to know 'Where do we go from here?' Or as onetime TUC general secretary George Woodcock might have put it: 'What are we here for?' Enough of them were out to put 'teeth' into that document to ensure a conference punch-up.

Maybe the TUC General Council couldn't avoid holding the conference but they really couldn't hope to march their troops up to the top of the hill and then expect them to step on to Cloud Nine and float peacefully away; now they are stuck with a one-day strike they didn't bargain for and most of them didn't want. And the TUC is due to 'organise and head co-ordinated action'. The overall resentment against the Government is thoroughly genuine and had to find some form of militant expression, I suppose. It's limited action but I find it hard to see it having any major effect on the situation. Moreover, it is clear that some of the union leaders I spoke to are worried that they will not secure the necessary response from their members to make the protest sufficiently successful. If it goes wrong it's a bonus to Heath.

The only other observer-MP there appeared to be Reg Prentice although two or three other MPs were at the Congress as members of their union delegations.

Back in the Commons, the debate on the Government's Pay and Prices Code was under way but it seemed a tame affair after the confused excitement of the Central Hall. That was where the more important decision of the day on the industrial front was taken.

6th, Tuesday: The House is always packed for the Budget and was today. Sir Gerald Nabarro, No. 1 Tory exhibitionist, had his topper on and Charles Simeons, the Tory from the traditional hatters town of Luton, wore a straw boater. One or two of the Tory women Members had also turned out in their best titfers.

Chancellor Barber gave a marathon two hour performance, impressive in presentation though hardly so in content. He called it 'neutral' – which I later found described in the dictionary as 'a state of indifference'. I shall use that phrase to describe it sometime soon.

The first half of the speech was listened to silently. No one expects much at the outset other than a sermon and that's what we got. It was all about economic growth, countering inflation and the need for prudence. Good Treasury stuff.

Then came the announcements. Not many surprises. VAT at 10 per cent as expected, with exemptions for some children's clothes and shoes and zero rating for sweets, crisps and soft drinks. Rises in pensions and related benefits, limited action to curb profiteering from North Sea oil, inducements to save if you've got any cash to spare and a very inadequate gesture called a 'land hoarding charge' which won't really get at the land and property sharks at all.

Nothing much to really help the Government sell its counter-inflation policy to the unions and to working people generally. The new unified tax system is to go ahead which means big concessions to the high-paid and those with investment income. No increase in family allowance. Certainly no question of cushioning the rise of essential foodstuffs or freezing the next round of rent rises.

Barber will probably get a good Press tomorrow but if he does it will show that a superficial judgment has been passed.

7th, Wednesday: Barber's Press was no more than fair to middling, not as sympathetic as I had anticipated. He certainly got no sympathy at our special Parliamentary Party meeting this morning to chew over our approach during the three days of Budget debate to come.

Dick Taverne duly took his Commons seat this afternoon. It should have been treated by us as a bit of a non-event if we wanted to be clever. But MPs are human enough. They all wanted a bird's-eye view and the Chamber was very full.

Two Labour MPs, Andrew Faulds and Dick Crawshaw, walked from the Bar of the House to the Mace and Table, one either side of Taverne. That solved the mystery of who would sponsor his re-entry to the Commons. Both are pro-Marketeers. Both are regarded as somewhat eccentric politically. But there is particular illwill abroad over Andrew, the actor-MP who is our Front Bench spokesman on the arts. It is felt that his official job is hardly compatible with sponsorship of a man who fought and beat an official Labour Parliamentary candidate. Personally, I am inclined to blame Taverne more than Faulds for this. If friendship really counted he would surely have prevented a demonstration that can only mean trouble.

Joe Ashton, the Bassetlaw MP who campaigned in Lincoln against Taverne for three weeks, threw his Order Paper towards

Faulds and stalked out of the Chamber. It was a bit over-dramatic but his temper was understandable.

If Harold Wilson sacks Andrew the Press will raise a howl of victimisation and complain about using the big stick. If he does nothing he will probably be accused of weakness. As usual, he can't hope to win. I think he should play it cool.

I met a large group of teachers, many of them from my constituency, in an upstairs Committee room for another chat about their claim for a bigger London allowance. They are all on strike. They are by no means habitual militants. Just sick of seeing their living standards sag. But I had to tell them that all Labour MPs could now do was to keep making a noise on their behalf. Until we get a change of Government.

Later I negotiated some awful traffic jams to keep a date at Ambler Primary School in my constituency and talk to retired teachers about my work as a MP. It's a subject which I am finding interests people enormously and leads to endless questions at sessions like this one – questions which I hope this book will help answer.

8th, Thursday: Britain looks in a hell of a mess today. The locomen are now on national one-day strike, with more to come, and London has been one huge traffic jam. Gas workers, London teachers, hospital ancillary workers, are still out too. Car workers and civil servants are planning further action. The miners' pay position looks decidely dodgy again.

I returned to the House from a lunch appointment and as I went into the Members' cloakroom there was dull crump which seemed to shake the building slightly. It was one of the two IRA bomb blasts – one at the Old Bailey and other in Whitehall – which killed a man and injured more than 200 people.

Inside the Chamber, a grim and grey-looking Robert Carr, the Home Secretary, deplored the outrages and drew complete support from all the MPs there. Later at our evening Parliamentary Party meeting, Harold Wilson said we would table a motion expressing our condemnation of the bombers.

I was due to meet a bunch of students from Harlow Technical College's Journalism Department to talk to them about my job. Because of the traffic jams due to the strike and the bombings, they eventually got to the House more than an hour late. It wasn't their day. On the way to an interview room, half of them got stuck in a lift. One turned out to be a trainee reporter from the Wisbech Advertiser, a paper I worked for briefly a good many years ago in the Fenland town where I met my wife.

Our communications working party met under Tony Benn tonight. We had a long and rather inconclusive discussion on the Press. But there were some valuable ideas floated and we may yet come up with something of a policy. Any worthwhile reform will meet immense Fleet Street hostility and, as Tony succinctly put it: 'How do we get the Press we want with the Press we've got?' All the more reason for being pretty sure of our ground before we move.

9th, Friday: 'Surgery' was brief tonight which was just as well as I had a 'report-back' meeting, too – one of that series of public sessions I hold for constituents every so often around my wards. This one, in Newington Green School, pulled in just over 40 people – not so bad since there was no burning local issue to inspire them to leave their tellys.

I got Evelyn Denington along to give her an additional platform for the GLC election campaign. There was no shortage of questions and it was gratifying to note that it was a genuine *public* meeting with very few of the audience being known Party workers.

10th, Saturday: The papers reported, verbatim in *The Times* and *Guardian*, a speech in Oxford by Roy Jenkins, dismissing the idea of a third political force, a new centre party, but sharply criticising the Labour Party for a 'slide to weakness' in the past two years. As always there is a great deal in Roy's contentions. But he doesn't tell the whole story.

He spurred me into writing my Labour Weekly column in defence of what I dubbed 'the third force inside the Labour Party – those who hold the middle ground'. I said they are not social democrats, but democratic socialists. They want to change the basis of society but accept they must persuade the electorate of their case before they can make major advances. I pointed to

Roy's assertion that we must represent the leftward thinking half of the country and suggested this hardly squared with support for Common Market entry imposed over the heads of the British people by a Tory Government; I added that the third force or so-called 'soft centre' has to be relied upon to make the Party a viable, sensible yet still idealistic, election-winning outfit – or it just won't happen.

Someone will doubtless see this piece as a heartcry for Harold Wilson. It's not intended as that. Nor as an attack on anyone either. It's just a necessary reminder to those on the more extreme wings of the Party that the 'soft centre' could just as aptly be named the 'hard core' and in the end is all-important.

12th, Monday: The Government's long-awaited White Paper on the future of broadcasting was published today – the formal reply to the report last August of the all-party Select Committee on Nationalised Industries' concerning the Independent Broadcasting Authority.

It was generally anticipated that the Government would extend until 1981 the BBC Charter and the Television Act governing independent television and would reject the Committee's call for a wide-ranging inquiry. This proved to be the case.

There was also considerable fear that Sir John Eden, the Posts and Telecommunications Minister, would also announce that the fourth TV channel would be allocated to commercial interests. But Eden disclosed that no decision has yet been reached on that.

He was due to answer questions in the Commons and used the opportunity to briefly disclose the salient features of his White Paper. MPs were able to collect copies of the White Paper at 2.30 p.m. as the Minister got up to speak. It meant they had no chance to read it in advance of Question Time, a ridiculous inhibition. Yet the Press are known to get copies of these documents well in advance, under embargo so that nothing is printed until the time fixed by the Minister – in this case, 2.30 p.m. to coincide with his Commons remarks. It's helpful and desirable for journalists to have copies prior to publication – but why not MPs? It's a matter I have raised previously in the House but only ever received a dusty answer.

There was considerable hostility to Eden's statement from our

Benches and I came in for the Opposition to denounce his White Paper as 'a tragedy of missed opportunity'. I said the Committee's central recommendation for an inquiry had been flouted and expressed my anxiety about the fourth channel. Eden stonewalled rather unhappily and we shall want an early debate on all this which the Government may well try to duck.

It was a busy day on the Floor of the House. Shadow Home Secretary Mrs Shirley Williams, undoubtedly ahead of the field if we are ever to have a woman Prime Minister, quizzed Home Secretary Robert Carr about the bomb outrage last week.

There was a statement from the Foreign Secretary, Sir Alec Douglas Home, who has managed to turn a key Cabinet post into a Parliamentary backwater. He dealt with the shock assassination of Sir Richard Sharples. the former Tory MP who became Governor General of Bermuda. I talked with Sharples once or twice on constituency cases while he was a Minister at the Home Office; he struck me as a pleasant, courteous but unimpressive man. On a grim occasion like today's, however, there were understandably warm and sympathetic tributes paid from both sides of the House.

We moved on to the final stages of the protracted Budget debate. But I had a meeting of the Party's Greater London Regional Council to attend as well as the broadcasting White Paper to study in rather more detail.

13th, Tuesday: The Prime Minister really did get rattled at Question Time today. He tried unsuccessfully to debunk the now inevitably staccato statistical attack which Michael Meacher launches to good purpose from our Backbenches. It doesn't always work for Michael but this time he was on food prices and Heath looked petty in contesting figures which are public knowledge. Then he came off second best in a clash with Harold Wilson over the threatened rise in mortgage interest rates.

I met two leading Swedish journalists – a husband and wife team – visiting Britain with the backing of Swedish Premier Olaf Palme as part of a 12-country tour to study employment policy for older workers. I went to Sweden with Expenditure Committee members last year and looked at their employment policy. It was generally far in advance of ours and I had to tell my visitors that I doubted if we had much to teach them. So they went on to interview me about the current strike situation. We can teach them a bit about strikes just now.

15th, Thursday: This morning I took part in a recorded television discussion with Julian Critchley, Secretary of the Tory Backbenchers' Broadcasting Committee, to go out on Anglia TV. We went to the ITN London studios for our argument over the Government's White Paper on broadcasting.

Heath was short-tempered again at Question Time, most noticeably when Harold Wilson justifiably pressed him about French nuclear testing in the Pacific. Presumably the cares and strains of office, particularly the industrial troubles and Ulster, are taking their toll.

Every Thursday immediately after Prime Minister's Questions the Leader of the House, currently James Prior, announces next week's Commons business and replies to questions about it. I had asked Harold Wilson to press for a full debate on broadcasting soon since the request would clearly carry far more weight coming from him than from me. He did so and Prior acknowledged the need with surprising readiness, although it will plainly not be yet awhile.

There was a minor blow-up inside our Parliamentary Party meeting, ASLEF, the locomen's union, has no sponsored MP. Less Huckfield, the Member for Nuneaton, supports their cause and has criticised the Party previously for not doing likewise quite openly. But the locomen's action is undoubtedly unpopular with Labour MPs as well as with the public. Many of our MPs are anxious to steer clear of a dispute that has inter-union undertones and also fear it will adversely hit the Labour vote in the forthcoming local government elections if it drags on much longer.

Huckfield, nothing daunted, had a smack at Reg Prentice for his public appeal the other day to the locomen to return to work. But the mood of the meeting was against Huckfield. Walter 'Johnny' Johnson, treasurer of the Transport Salaried Staffs' Association, the rail clerks' union, who is MP for Derby South, virtually told him to keep his nose out of rail union business and warned the Party that cool heads are needed while delicate behind-the-scenes efforts to resolve the dispute are going on.

Johnny is sponsored by his union which means that his Constituency Party gets an annual grant from the union to help meet its expenses and inevitably an additional lump sum at election times. There are probably around 100 sponsored MPs in the House currently.

16th, Friday: The 'surgery' lasted about two hours. There were the usual housing cases. One distressed mother, living in appalling damp conditions, brought a plastic bag full of mildewed clothing to show me just how bad things are for her.

There was an old gent who wanted me to draw up his will. I sent him on for legal help. There was a young actress with a United States passport – in effect, an accident of birth-place since her parents had travelled widely and she has lived the past eight years in Britain. She needed aid over naturalisation papers.

There is very limited political kudos in running an advice bureau. The word filters around that you do so and for every constituent that you are able to help, there are probably two more that end up as dissatisfied customers. Some of them don't even give you marks for trying.

Some MPs only hold fortnightly or even monthly 'surgeries'. If the casework doesn't demand more frequency, if they have far distant constituencies, or if they perhaps have heavy Ministerial responsibilities, there is no cause to complain. But some hold none at all or leave it entirely to their Party agent or local councillors. They seem to get away with it.

Most Members appear to be fairly conscientious in dealing with correspondence. But I heard of one MP, now dead, who had his own golden rule. He never answered a constituent's letter until he got a second one, asking him why he hadn't replied. That way, a large number of queries simply melt away, doubtless an effective way of reducing the workload. But running a 'surgery' and handling a postbag properly would seem to me to be part of my unwritten contract of employment. That apart, they play an important part in keeping you in touch with your electorate and knowing firsthand their opinions and their problems.

20th, Tuesday: Northern Ireland was all-important this afternoon. The White Paper on the future of the province was published and Willie Whitelaw, the Secretary of State for Northern Ireland, made a Commons statement describing it as 'a reasonable deal for reasonable people'. It proposed elections and a new assembly this year. I wish Whitelaw well but it will doubtless be the unreasonable people who will make the running again.

Whitelaw promised a full debate next week and although there was instant criticism from Independent MPs Miss Bernadette Devlin and Frank McManus, both rare Parliamentary performers these days, the Labour Opposition was restrained. The real argument will break out when the terms of the document have been studied.

The Government deliberately and sensibly refrained from giving any advance warning of precisely when it intended to publish the White Paper so that the bombers and troublemakers would not be alerted. Security at the House was extra tight. More police on duty and more questioning of people entering the building.

I had a visit from the CPSA's Bill Kendall to discuss his union's latest position on strike action over their outstanding pay claim. He waited for me in the Central Lobby for about ten minutes and noticed that someone had left a handbag unattended on a seat for some while. My initial inclination was to laugh it off as an unduly alarmist reaction. But I had second thoughts and reported it to the nearest policeman as a precaution.

21st, Wednesday: One of my constituency organisations, the Kerridge Court and Hawthorne Close Tenants, asked me along to say a few words at the opening of a community room on their housing estate. They had laid on tea for quite a few old people who told me how pleased they were to be able to get together in this way. It sounds incredible but I was told that for one old lady it was her first outing in more than 20 years.

London teachers had a one-day protest strike on; back at the House I had yet another session with a group from Islington – at least the third time I have discussed their pay claim with them recently. It's Tories they need to chase and I suggested they should press the Tory GLC candidates to state publicly their views on the issue.

In the Chamber there was a debate on the strike by low-paid hospital workers. Sir Keith Joseph, the Social Services Minister, rejected Labour demands for an independent inquiry and insisted that the Government could not allow special cases. Dick Taverne made his 'maiden' speech following his return to the House. I missed it but it was apparently marked primarily by his exchanges with two of his bitterest Labour critics, Joe Ashton and Denis Skinner. Taverne irked them particularly by insisting that a Labour Government would have to introduce a statutory incomes policy. The simple answer to that is that the last Labour Government found it necessary to abandon just such a policy as impracticable. Taverne as a junior member of that Government knows all about that first hand and seems to be one of the few ex-Ministers of that period to have failed to have learned the lesson. A statutory approach will only be workable, outside of dire emergencies, if the unions themselves opt for an incomes policy and ultimately seek help to deal with their own 'rogue elephants'. That day, if it ever comes, is a long long way off.

Tonight Islington Central Labour Party held its annual meeting. I said a bit about the need to secure a handsome win in the GLC election – 'a tremendous blow to the Tories, a tremendous boost to us and a signal to the nation'. It was a packed meeting which suggests rightly that we aren't short of active members. But the overall Party membership figures for the past year don't show the kind of big increase we ought to achieve in a period of abysmal Tory Government and I felt obliged to make that point even though a few folk there might not like it.

23rd, Friday: A woman broke down in a state of great distress tonight at my 'surgery' as she described her housing problem. She wasn't really in bad conditions. It was the noise in the area that troubled her. She became near-hysterical and went off sobbing. She clearly needs a move. Although she will get some consideration on medical grounds, the overall assessment of her need has already brought a rejection of her plea for rehousing and I can't see much chance of shifting that.

There was a case too, where another woman looked pretty close to tears. This time, because there are children involved, I think a bit of pressure may bring a more favourable outcome.

After about 90 minutes I was through and went on to a pensioners' meeting at Islington Town Hall. The gathering had been called by the local branch of the Old Age Pensions Associations' Federation to try and persuade more organisations in the borough to co-operate in helping the pensioners' cause. There was a lot of talk of militancy which was entirely understandable but insufficient constructive discussion of just how organisations could do more to aid pensioners with their day-to-day on-the-spot difficulties.

25th, Sunday: There was a very good reception on the doorsteps this morning when I canvassed for the GLC election. One encouraging aspect which I noticed was the way in which people responded with recognition (and, for the most part, with approval!) when I introduced myself. It certainly wasn't possible to get that sort of reaction in 1970 when I canvassed for my own candidature at the General Election.

26th, Monday: No more private beds in new hospitals and the phasing out of existing private beds by the next Labour Government. This promise was made from our Front Bench by Dr Shirley Summerskill in a debate on National Health Service re-organisation. That's exactly the kind of commitment that needs to be made.

27th, Tuesday: I had a quick dig at Maurice Macmillan during Employment questions. He dealt with the strike by hospital workers and I asked him why he showed 'appalling intransigence' in dealing with this case involving lowpaid workers yet allowed the recent newspaper industry settlement. Macmillan, doubtless recalling our brush over this at last month's Standing Committee, looked uncomfortable but parried by saying I should table a specific question if I sought details.

My schedule was pretty tight for the rest of the day: 4.30 p.m., meeting of the Parliamentary Party Communications Group to discuss the Broadcasting White Paper; 5.30 p.m., special Parliamentary Party meeting to approve the Shadow Cabinet line for the following two days of debate on the Government's Northern Ireland proposals; 6 p.m., a Fabian working party meeting on industrial relations.

Then a quick egg on toast and off to Islington for more GLC doorstep electioneering, this time in a huge estate of tower blocks overlooking the Arsenal Stadium. Again there was a generally good reception.

I was back in the House soon after 9 p.m. in good time for the vote at the end of the two-days debate on the National Health Service.

I drove home intending to watch the Warhol film that was finally on the TV screen after the long controversy and legal action. I missed the start, watched about 15 minutes or so, then dozed off in the armchair. What little I saw seemed monumentally boring – which is what I told the reporter who rang me at midnight for a comment.

29th, Thursday: I fitted in a quick game of squash at lunchtime, got some friends, together with my wife, into the public gallery, and listened to questions to the Prime Minister and to the Leader of the House about forthcoming business. This time, the Leader, James Prior, gave a commitment to Harold Wilson that he will arrange a debate on broadcasting soon after Easter. It should be my first opportunity to make a speech from the Despatch Box.

I remained for Harold Wilson's opening remarks in the Ulster debate. We have no Party Whip on this but the vast bulk of the Parliamentary Labour Party will give uneasy support to the Government's White Paper proposals if maverick Ulster Unionist MPs force a vote as seems probable. 'Give it a try', is the Labour Party line.

I left the House to do a quick BBC broadcast debate with Tory stockbroker MP Peter Tapsell. Subject: the economy. I was back in Westminster in time for the weekly Parliamentary Party meeting which turned out to be uneventful.

The Tories had kept a safe majority of their MPs around to ensure that the anticipated 'rebel' vote at 10 o'clock would be crushed. Many of our MPs went off but I decided to stay behind and put my view on the record. It was another of those rare occasions when I found myself literally rubbing shoulders with

Heath in the same voting lobby. The Government duly got its overwhelming majority.

30th, Friday: The Government has not kept me posted, as promised, on its inquiries into computer training schools. I have had no positive response and have tired of waiting so have decided to try and 'take the lid' off by talking to the *Sunday Times*. A reporter came to see me at home. I passed over to him all the relevant documents; he will start an investigation and come back to me before anything is published.

'Surgery' tonight took two hours. One woman wanted to discuss a 15-year-old murder case, there was a father seeking help in securing compensation for what seemed to be a thalidomide child, and the other constituents included two from blocks of flats where homeless families are being temporarily housed. Some of them are problem families and their noise and general behaviour is clearly causing distress and grave strains to the long-standing residents who are eventually due to be rehoused when the flats are redeveloped. I have had allegations of prostitution, drug-taking, break-ins and even the regular theft of women's underwear from clothes lines. Tenants have told me they are frightened to let their children out to play.

Tonight's two complaints make a total of five from the same flats in just a few weeks and the stories roughly tally. The people who have been to see me all seem decent hardworking types with genuine worries. The damp and depressing condition of the flats adds to the need for action.

I shall have a look at them and then take up the whole issue with the Council. Many of these homeless families are unable to integrate and be good neighbours, hence the tension. It looks as though the Council was mistaken to move them in in this way. Yet the Council can't win. If it fails to house homeless families, it is branded as heartless and evading its responsibilities. It is one more example of the grotesque pressure on inner city areas like Islington which is unable to get other more fortunate areas to carry a fair share of the burden.

I finished the 'surgery' with a deputation of nursery school nurses worried about their future careers under new Government plans for nursery education. They seemed bright girls and several of them were pretty. We had a useful chat about the need for them to join a union. They have already written to both Mrs Margaret Thatcher, the Education Minister, and Sir Keith Joseph, the Social Services Minister, and when they have got replies they will contact me again to see if I can take things any further for them. They were grateful that someone had listened to their arguments. Until now they had felt ignored.

April

1st, Sunday: This morning's GLC election canvass was in a Holloway Ward council estate and once more the reception was good. Getting them out to vote will be the problem though.

I went home via Marble Arch so that I could call at an hotel there and pick up a friend from the Swedish TUC who is over here on a short visit. He had lunch with us at home – his first taste of Yorkshire pudding. One particular impression he left with me was that the Government's proposals to modernise our employment services on Swedish lines, cutting out the old 'dole queue' image by introducing swish new open-plan offices and so on, are well worthwhile but already out of date by Swedish standards. There they are moving on with their active labour market policy and getting their employment officers involved first-hand in the factories over both redundancy and recruitment.

2nd, Monday: It was my turn on the Front Bench again to deal with broadcasting questions for the Opposition. But there were only a handful on the subject due for reply and I went to the Despatch Box briefly and only once.

Later I went to a reception at the West German Embassy to mark the opening of the German Television Festival. There was a fair sprinkling of British broadcasting personalities around. They included Charles Curran, the BBC's Director-General, with whom I had a useful chat about his organisation's views on the 4th TV Channel.

I went from the Embassy to the National Film Theatre to see excerpts from a selection of German TV films. One of them recorded the proceedings in the West German Parliament when Chancellor Brandt faced a crisis vote of confidence. It was the kind of historic occasion which British TV should be able to record and the public here should be able to watch.

3rd, Tuesday: I had a question down to Heath about the Pay and Price Code and intended to twit him about that recent newspaper industry settlement. But my question was No. 8 on the Order Paper. We ran out of time at No. 7.

Heath had received a fillip. The miners' ballot, announcing a substantial majority against strike action over their pay claim, had just been announced. He wore his cat-with-the-cream look when one of his own Backbenchers teed up a question to him about it.

On the other hand, he is in trouble over building society borrowing rates and looks unlikely to be able to prevent an increase. That will upset home-owners and be a blow to the Tories on the eve of the local government elections.

Heath sniped at Harold Wilson over Labour's support for the TUC May Day strike idea and Harold snapped back at him about those mortgage rates. I doubt if either of them ended up feeling very satisfied.

London MPs had a meeting with representatives of the Police Federation, the policemen's trade union, at which the serious problem of shrinking police manpower in the Metropolitan area was sharply underlined. There was a useful exchange of views and the Federation, which has made little headway with the Home Secretary, clearly gained understanding and sympathy for their case from MPs like myself who had not been fully aware of the current state of play. Some further pressure on the Government should result from this meeting.

Tonight I went electioneering again, this time in Highbury Ward. I was canvassing private terraced properties. Quite a few of them were occupied by immigrants who will certainly back Labour if they trouble to cast their votes. I think they are gradually becoming more conscious of the need to do so.

4th, Wednesday: I kept a longstanding commitment tonight to speak at a Beckenham Labour Party meeting – part of their effort in the GLC contest.

Beckenham Party selected me to fight the 1966 General Election, my first taste of Parliamentary candidature. I was genuinely surprised to be chosen at the time but, although there was a huge Tory majority to combat, it was a Party with willing helpers, plenty of spirit and with far better organisation than you sometimes find in so-called 'safe' Labour seats. Anyway, it produced a campaign which I thoroughly enjoyed and from which I learned a lot.

Those mortgage interest rates are to go up so I said a bit to the meeting about that, dealt with a few of the specific GLC issues but pointed out that most people would vote primarily on the activities of the parties nationally and would, I hoped, pay special attention to the Government's failure to hold prices.

5th, Thursday: If I get any further complaints like those last Friday about those wretched flats, I shall be able to say that things are no longer static.

I had a lengthy talk on the telephone earlier in the week with the Borough Housing Manager, Miss Muriel Mayell. She was well aware of the position and sympathetic. Her very real dilemma: if she moved out tenants without filling up the vacated flats with homeless families, squatters may move in. That could mean a further headache. But it can't just be shelved and I made it plain that if necessary I should have to make an outcry. I got a phone call back today to say the Council would soon be starting again on moving tenants out. So the beginnings of a solution for the worst-hit families is in sight.

What a day for the Government in the House. They really took a hammering.

First of all Labour MPs had a real romp, largely at the expense of Mrs Peggy Fenner, the junior Minister from Agriculture. She had to admit that a 3 lb. chicken had risen 30 per cent in price since the General Election even though the price remained unchanged throughout the previous six years of Labour Government. She got similar rough treatment over the price of eggs and cheese.

Then Heath was rapidly thrown on the defensive over the mortgage interest rate rises. Harold Wilson taunted him by holding up a copy of the Tory Party Manifesto and asking pertinently: 'Is Mr 9½–10 per cent any relation to the author of this book in 1970 in which he said he will reverse the decline of building and make home ownership easier and concentrate Government subsidies where they are needed?'

There was far worse to come.

Geoffrey Rippon, the usually unflappable Environment Minister, had the dread task of making a statement to the House about the interest rates and the Government's panic decision to give a £15 million handout to the building societies to keep the rise down to 1 per cent over the next three months. First Tony Crosland, then Harold Wilson, from our Front Bench, ridiculed Rippon. Roy Jenkins suggested the £15 million should come from Tory Party funds since it was intended as a sop to the local government electors.

Behind Rippon his own MPs looked suitably chastened. The now-familiar stab in the back came from Enoch Powell. 'Is there any longer anything which this Government is not prepared to subsidise?', he asked.

One solitary Tory MP, James Allason, did his best. He suggested a lot of people warmly support the Government's action. If that is so they certainly weren't around the Commons, even on the Tory Benches, to judge from the rows of miserable faces.

The Parliamentary Party tonight received a verbal report from our chairman, Douglas Houghton, from the special committee set up under Deputy Leader Ted Short to consider the matter of Members' outside interests. We shall get our copies of the report in the post tomorrow. The report favours a register, together with a Code of Conduct which would make it more certain than at present that Members would declare outside cash interests they have or might have related to any Parliamentary proceedings they are involved in or even when writing to Ministers or civil servants. The Code would have to be agreed by the whole House but Douglas made it clear that a register could be kept by us if the Tories dissent (I later heard that their Backbenchers met tonight and cold shouldered the scheme).

We will debate the register at a future Party meeting soon. But the proposals seem to me to contain shortcomings. Most important, they suggest that the register would be open only to the officers of the Party for inspection or – if the Tories did back the plan – to the Speaker. Yet if the public is to feel really assured, justice must not only be done but be seen to be done. We can count on a robust debate on all this before any verdict is reached.

6th, Friday: A steady queue and more than two hours 'surgery' tonight. Try this for variation:

a petition from tenants of a block of flats complaining about inadequate maintenance, three more distressed tenants of those flats where the homeless families have been rehoused, a tax problem, a couple more would-be housing transfer cases, a race relations complaint involving alleged unfair dismissal, a plea for help from the mother of a disabled girl unable to get a replacement for her out-of-action invalid car, a resident's protest about the 'goings-on' at a local youth centre and a heartcry from the wife of a man jailed for armed robbery – a loyal and plaintive insistence on his innocence.

7th, Saturday: I drove, with Miles, to Sheffield, to see the FA Cup Semi-Final between Arsenal and Sunderland. We started with a flat tyre, hit a mammoth traffic jam on the M.1 because two out of the three lanes were closed a bit south of Sheffield, had no time to get lunch and on the way back heavy rain made driving most unpleasant. Between times Arsenal lost 1–2 so it was not the most successful of outings.

8th, Sunday: Another morning's canvassing. It was all in council flats, rock-solid for Labour. But there were one or two folk who said they wouldn't vote at all because 'You're all the same.' One said he was a staunch trade unionist who didn't like the way Labour handled the unions but was also disenchanted with our failure to send representatives to the European Parliament now Britain was in the Common Market. I was able to tell him I agreed with him on both issues and have consistently said so. I think he'll come back to us but not necessarily at this GLC election.

9th, Monday: Lunch at the House with three Commonwealth MPs – one from Australia and two from the West Indies. They are all attending a seminar arranged by the Commonwealth Parliamentary Association which brings together MPs throughout the Commonwealth to exchange views and information. These MPs had been in daily conference every day for two weeks, week-ends apart, and certainly agreed that their trip was no junket.

My overseas visits so far have been limited to a trip to Norway in 1971, which I fixed up on a purely personal basis through the Norwegian Government, to look at industrial relations there, and a week in Sweden last year with members of the Expenditure Committee for a firsthand sight of their employment policy in operation. Foreign visits can be vastly overrated in their value and some MPs do seem to cram in quite a few without any apparent return accruing to Parliament here. But those who go with open and inquiring minds, prepared to work and learn, can gain a lot from these exchanges.

During the past week-end I put out a brief statement about Peter Niesewand, the journalist jailed for two years in Rhodesia, following a secret trial. Apart from my general condemnation, I suggested that the world's Press might do something more tangible than just protest by using their resources to expose 'sanctions-busters' in their respective countries since widespread evasion of trade sanctions against Rhodesia is acknowledged by the British Government.

Heath faced a Private Notice Question from Harold Wilson on this today. This device enables a Member to raise a particularly urgent matter immediately after the normal Question Time, providing the Speaker agrees in advance. An on-the-spot Ministerial reply is required. It is unusual for an Opposition Leader to table a 'PNQ' but feeling on the Niesewand affair is running high.

Harold Wilson lashed into the Rhodesian regime. There was no attempt to score party points from either side of the House. Indeed, several Tories were scathing in their attacks on Ian Smith, the Rhodesian leader. Heath was unable to offer much hope of moving the immovable but I was pleased that Harold Wilson picked up my point about the world's Press and commended it to the Prime Minister.

We got back to the partisan stuff pretty quickly, however. Environment Minister Geoffrey Rippon announced his plans to curb land hoarding and then a major debate on mortgages began. Tony Crosland saw the Government's inadequate efforts as a bribe to the electors prior to Thursday's local government polling. No doubt about that. Rippon was laughed at, loud and long, when he sought to deny it. His own Backbenchers looked most unhappy.

10th, Tuesday: This morning I tabled a question to Sir Keith Joseph, the Social Services Minister, asking him to speed up the provision of replacement invalid cars to disabled people whose own vehicles are being repaired. I have had two cases recently where disabled constituents have had long waits and only gained temporary replacement vehicles after letters from me to the Minister. But there seems to be something wrong with the system that needs looking at.

There was a noisy slanging match at Prime Minister's questions. Heath accused Harold Wilson of misleading everyone over the Labour Government's Common Market entry terms. Harold told him: 'It's a lie.' That's a word that's regarded as un-Parliamentary. The Speaker intervened and Harold withdrew it. He adroitly substituted 'pack of lies' which the Chancellor of the Exchequer apparently used recently without being stopped.

You have to be careful if you feel abusive. Not long ago, someone called a Member opposite 'half drunk', was pulled up, withdrew the remark and substituted 'half sober'. But that was ruled out too.

11th, Wednesday: I spent the morning at Broadcasting House, talking to some of the key people at the BBC, then lunched with the Director-General, Charles Curran. It was a good opportunity to clear my mind on some of the matters I shall hope to raise during the debate on broadcasting which now seems likely to come up on the day the House resumes after the Easter recess.

Back at Westminster the Chamber was already packed when I arrived. Tories, out to restore the death penalty, were backing a 10-minute rule Bill advanced by a Backbencher, Teddy Taylor. If the House approved, the Bill would have crossed the first hurdle towards becoming law, although the chances of such a controversial measure progressing far without formal Government backing would be remote.

The advance propaganda for this Bill had been considerable and hardly justified by the public mood so far as I can tell. Right-wing newspapers have done their best to whip up a bit of hysteria. But I asked a random half dozen or so of my colleagues what their postbags showed and, other than Shirley Williams, the Shadow Home Secretary, few of them had received a single letter on the issue and none more than one letter. The one letter I got was from a rather surprising source – a local Baptist Minister who actually quoted 'an eye for an eye' at me. I was unable to please him with my reply or my vote.

For these Bills, the mover gets 10 minutes and a Member is allowed 10 minutes to oppose. Taylor's view was contested by Roy Jenkins, one time Labour Home Secretary, who apparently got the job of putting the anti-hanging case from the Speaker because he was first in the queue.

The turnout, on this free voting occasion, was most impressive, especially since many MPs were expected to be away in their constituencies to help in the local election campaign.

Taylor lost by 320 to 178. His vote comprised of one hundred and seventy-four Tories and Ulster Unionists, three Labour MPs and the Scottish Nationalist. So Taylor tested Commons opinion and lost decisively, although he could claim that the Government, which was not in favour of reopening the issue, was sustained by Labour votes, with only seventy-nine Tories against him.

It was certainly a rare experience to be voting in the same lobby as Messrs. Heath, Wilson, Thorpe and Powell. Perhaps never to be repeated.

12th, Thursday: Most of the day was spent cruising around the constituency with a loudspeaker fixed on the car, urging people to vote Labour. Pat drove and David was the backseat driver.

By the time the polls closed at 9 o'clock I felt pretty hoarse. But it was worthwhile. We held all three Islington seats comfortably. Central Islington's Liberal challenger came bottom and appeared to pick up most of his votes from the Tories anyway.

It looks like a good omen for me at the General Election. But the most disturbing feature was that less than a third of the electors bothered to vote at all. Everyone had the impression that young people are not responding.

The best moment came at the Town Hall count as Evelyn Denington made a short speech of thanks on behalf of the winning Labour trio. She was just under way as the vital news came through that Labour had secured an overall majority on the GLC and had recaptured political control of London.

13th, Friday: The final GLC result: Labour 58, Tories 32, Liberals 2. It should be a real tonic for the Party. It was good to feel that I had made a positive contribution.

One thing emerges as a near-certainty after these results, which show a substantial swing to us all over the country: Heath will avoid any early General Election.

17th, Tuesday: Heath got bounced around a bit again at Question Time. He was asked about the launching of his new yacht which annoyed him. Then a trying-to-be-helpful Tory referred to the Prime Minister's recent remarks about the quiet people who don't protest or strike and support the Government line. Back came Pat Duffy, himself a quiet-spoken Labour Backbencher, to ask where all those quiet people were last Thursday when they might have been expected to be voting for the Tories at the local elections.

The main debate was on Ulster and the Government's Bill to replace the Special Powers Act. The Shadow Cabinet advice to Labour MPs was to abstain because although there is anxiety about continuing internment without trial, there is also reluctance to deny the Government its emergency legislation in the prevailing Northern Ireland situation.

I gathered that the Republican Ulster MPs and a few of our Backbenchers would force a division against the Government. It is physically impossible to keep abreast of all the legislation going through the House. I hadn't studied this Bill in detail and decided to accept the Shadow Cabinet line even though, on a previous Ulster vote bearing some similarity to this one in respect of the issue, I had rejected the same advice and voted with a group of other Labour MPs against the Government. That time though, I had listened carefully to the debate, originally intending to back the Government. But I found myself thoroughly unconvinced by their case and – at the last minute – changed my mind and opposed.

Tonight I left before the vote to pay a visit on my way home to the Ravensbourne Labour Party's meeting. This is in my home area where I am a Party member, was an activist for many years and local Party chairman for some four years. Despite my priority allegiance to Islington, I still try and attend occasionally since there is no Labour MP in the area. I made a short speech and answered questions. One thing that seemed to come across from them was a feeling that we ought to be represented in the European Parliament.

18th, Wednesday: I was in the House well before lunchtime to check my mail and keep a lunch date in the Press Gallery. Which was just as well. Bob Mellish, the Chief Whip, wanted me to speak from the Front Bench for us on a statement to be made this afternoon by Posts Minister Sir John Eden. It was about electronic telephone exchange equipment and was very much Gregor Mackenzie's subject but he was away and has no formal deputy.

That meant a spot of quick mugging up. But it was a non-controversial decision which the Government was announcing, supported by the Post Office unions, so I could welcome it.

First though, came that Gallery lunch. The Parliamentary journalists hold these functions regularly, invite prominent guest speakers and take guests along themselves. I was there in the latter capacity. The principal guest and speaker was Independent Broadcasting Authority chairman Lord Aylestone, formerly in the Commons as Herbert Bowden, a Labour Chief Whip.

The chairman at the lunch was Maurice Woods, like me a former industrial reporter. He is well known for his witty contributions and this time introduced Aylestone in verse which may sound corny but was extremely cleverly done. Aylestone responded by outlining the various pressures upon him and defending his IBA 'amateurs' vigorously.

In the Chamber, Eden made his statement and I asked him a few questions on points of detail. The mini-debate on this went on, rather surprisingly, for nearly half an hour. The Speaker would doubtless have called a halt more rapidly but we were on the verge of the Easter recess, there was no important matter to come and Members were clearly melting away already. The House formally goes into recess tomorrow but this, in effect, is it.

26th, Thursday: Going away for a few days with the family to stay with my in-laws at Ely, near Cambridge, made a welcome Easter break. But the mail was well piled up today when we got home.

Moreover, I shall have to put in a lot of preparatory work between now and Monday when the House resumes. I am speaking at a dinner on Saturday evening, must deal with Front Bench questions that may arise on broadcasting on Monday, and I am due to speak at a May Day protest meeting on Tuesday, a Labour Party meeting in Islington on Wednesday and must wind up for the Opposition on Thursday at the end of the long-awaited all-day debate on the Commons Select Committee's report on broadcasting. This latter speech will be my 'maiden' from the Front Bench, leaving aside Question Time contributions, and will also be the longest Commons speech I have made – I shall get the 30 minutes each customarily allocated to both the Government and Opposition Front Bench for winding up in major debates.

The Party leadership agrees that we ought to record our distaste for the Tory White Paper which replies so inadequately to the Select Committee report and I have drafted a suitably critical amendment to the expected Government motion to merely 'take note' of the report. We shall back the amendment on a two-line Whip.

27th, Friday: A busy two-hour 'surgery' tonight, mostly housing cases.

The *Sunday Times* was in touch for my final comments to round off its inquiries on the computer training schools affair. They hope to run a fairly detailed story this week-end. I told them I shall try to raise it all in the House more fully than before, probably by seeking an adjournment debate.

28th, Saturday: Pat and I were guests tonight at the North London Athletic Club dinner, held at Alexandra Palace. It was a pleasant and entirely social occasion and although I was called on to make a brief speech, I was able to be non-political and talk largely in lighter vein.

The Club draws some membership from my constituency area and also from Stationer's Company's School, Hornsey, where I was once a pupil. It was formed from a merger which took in the former Hornsey St Mary's Athletics Club of which I was once a member for a short time, although, as I said at the dinner, I have won more elections than races. Well, I have won one election. And it was pleasant to renew some old links.

29th, Sunday: The *Sunday Times* carried the computer training schools story today at quite some length. It explained my views, my attempts to push the Government into action and my intended Parliamentary effort to come. It said it had compiled its own dossier of case histories concerning students who have lost their course fees or deposits through being refused entry to Britain and supported my views fully.

I shall write to the Speaker soon asking for the debate. I shall be surprised though, if I don't get some reaction before that from various interested parties.

30th, Monday: It was my turn on the Front Bench again this afternoon (the first day back after the Easter recess) for questions to the Minister for Posts and Telecommunications. I intervened a couple of times but there was little that could be meaningfully said prior to Thursday's full debate on the subject. I also chipped in during questions to the Parliamentary Secretary to the Civil Service, Kenneth Baker, to register a further belated dig at the Government over the appointment of Tory Central Office men to work within Ministries.

The Party's Greater London Regional executive had its first gathering since the GLC election triumph and Sir Reg Goodwin, now top man at County Hall, made a characteristically modest speech, praising everyone for helping him to office.

May

1st, Tuesday: I was supposed to go to the BBC's Lime Grove studios to speak at a May Day meeting of the TV union members there. But the BBC apparently refused permission for the one-hour protest to take place on the premises. The unions hired a room at a nearby public house and allowing time for them getting there and back, it probably cost about 1½ hours production overall.

More than 100 employees turned up and I was told that Lime Grove was virtually at a standstill, although the meeting was called in the morning to avoid direct interference with programmes. I had a good reception and no adverse reaction when I said that I felt that a Labour Government would need to return to a voluntary incomes policy. Since many of those present were pretty well paid that seemed quite promising.

In the House later, Heath claimed that 85 per cent of trade unionists were at work despite the TUC invitation to stop for the day in protest at Government policies.

But the main interest was in a statement from Joe Godber, the Agriculture Minister, just back from negotiations over EEC farm prices and claiming a victory. Ministers usually provide the Opposition with an advance copy of Commons statements about half an hour before they make them. But Godber didn't have time to do so and Peter Shore, responding for us, got his preview only minutes before Godber got up. It was all rather too complex for most of us to understand adequately off-the cuff. But it was enough to cheer up the Government supporters, suffering from a series of defeats in the abortive Tory bid to maintain some sort of price control at home.

The Parliamentary Labour Party's Economic and Finance Group heard from Campbell Adamson, Director-General of the

Confederation of British Industry, at its private meeting. Adamson, an example of the more progressive CBI man, gave a good account of himself and fielded some hostile questions deftly.

I learned that the Government only intends to put up Sir John Eden to speak for it in Thursday's broadcasting debate. I discussed this with Gregor Mackenzie and then with Harold Wilson and we all agreed that we shouldn't respond to this effort to down-grade the importance of the debate. We will stick to two Front Bench speakers and it will probably mean that I will make the final speech before the vote, customarily the preserve of the Government.

2nd, Wednesday: I chaired an informal meeting of Labour MPs interested in taking part in tomorrow's broadcasting debate. Gregor Mackenzie and I gave an outline of the views we intended to express and so did Russell Kerr, the MP for Feltham who was chairman of the Select Committee probe into the Independent Broadcasting Authority and will open the debate from the Backbench since the Government motion refers directly to his Committee's report.

I was 'paired' for a couple of hours and went to speak in the constituency at a Highbury Ward Labour Party meeting. Subject: prices and pensions. Back to the House for a 10 o'clock vote, off to the Cafe Royal to a function held to mark the retirement of a senior television union official and then a dash back to the Commons again for a final vote at 11.30 p.m.

3rd, Thursday: It was the broadcasting debate today. I wouldn't say my nerves were too bad but I knew I should feel vastly relieved when it was over. Sitting through it all until the very end before I could speak myself was no help. It also meant that I had to be precise with my timing and ready to sit down just a few seconds before 10 p.m. so that the vote could take place. I had prepared a speech with enough spare material so that I didn't have to worry about drying up at the Despatch Box and I had also worked out what I could safely jettison if time was running out.

There were some good speeches even though the Chamber was

never very full. I felt bound to repeat some of the points made by other speakers earlier in the debate – inevitable when you are winding up. There had been very little said by the Government spokesman, Sir John Eden, which required me to alter the highly critical tone of my prepared speech.

I was rather tense when I got up. Yet the Despatch Box is oddly comforting. It gives you something to rest your papers on and something to grip. You don't need to worry, as you may from the Backbenches, about what to do with your hands – or at least the one not holding your notes if you use them, as most speakers do.

I ripped into the Government about as strongly as this unemotive subject would allow. I ended with a spirited attack on 'the Government of a commercially-sponsored Party' for seeking to decide the future of broadcasting in hole-in-the-corner fashion. By this time the attendance was quite respectable. Not that many Members had turned up to hear me. They were there in readiness for the 10 o'clock vote when I sat down.

Still, so far as I could tell my speech went well. Quite a few fellow MPs congratulated me afterwards and I believe and hope it was not entirely from comradeship or politeness.

6th, Sunday: I arrived in Margate for the Civil and Public Services Association's annual conference and spent the evening (until nearly 3 a.m., in fact) touring the hotels with several senior union officials to meet delegates. It is a big conference with more than 1,000 delegates. There are to be two guest speakers – Vic Feather, the TUC general secretary and myself. I am due to say my piece tomorrow.

7th, Monday: There is no doubt that my Parliamentary efforts on civil servants' pay have been well and truly noted by the CPSA membership and I received a genuinely warm reception when I got up to speak this afternoon.

Although I have made very few, I enjoy making a platform speech to a big audience. I seem to have developed a good natural sense of timing for these occasions or so I am told.

The union is non-political. Of those conferences delegates with a political alignment, the majority were probably Labour Party supporters. But there were undoubtedly a good many Tories and a lively sprinkling of International Socialists, Communist and various other fringe groups.

I handed out the kind of highly political anti-Government line which might have been frowned upon in other years and could have embarrassed the platform. Indeed, I was told that one angry Tory woman delegate did stamp out.

But the bulk of the conference was with me. I was supposed to speak for 20 minutes but hadn't allowed time for – and hadn't expected – the frequent applause which punctuated my remarks. I couldn't pretend that my points about incomes policy or even my delicately phrased mention of political affiliation – 'I wouldn't try to influence you against joining the Conservative Party' – were rapturously received. Neither, though, was there any real hostility. And when I drew to a close with a smack at 'a bloody unfair Government' the clapping was prolonged.

The first day of the conference was severely marred, however, by a subsequent decision to instruct civil servants not to pay out pensions rises until their own pay demands were met by Heath. The union leadership opposed the move and never really expected the 365 to 348 vote against them.

I told Bill Kendall, the CPSA general secretary, that I would do nothing to further that decision which conflicted sharply with my own campaigning for a better deal for pensioners. I said I felt like quitting as the union's Parliamentary consultant but I would wait and see what happened. There did seem to be a good chance that the decision would be reversed later in the week. The union's Posts and Telecommunications Section was absent at a separate meeting when the crucial vote was taken. We gathered that this Section would seek to have the vote rescinded when it joined the rest of the delegates on Wednesday.

8th, Tuesday: The pressure was starting to build up to get that pensions verdict quashed. So many delegates sought my view, and so did several journalists, that I issued a brief statement calling the decision 'a sorry mistake'.

I said that civil servants' bitterness over pay was understandable and especially in the Department of Health and Social

Security, which must deal with the increases, where there has long been an unduly heavy workload. But this decision could only hurt pensioners and was incompatible with union efforts to get them a decent living standard. I hoped 'wiser counsels will prevail'.

9th, Wednesday: I rate it valuable to spend a couple of days at a union conference talking about the problems facing not only the union top brass but also the ordinary delegates. I was 'paired' for Monday and Tuesday. Before returning to London, I put in an hour at the conference in anticipation of a further rumpus. The overnight rumours were proved correct.

First, the union president Len Lever refused to allow the pensions issue to be debated again during this same conference even though the Post Office delegates had been missing. He stuck to constitutional points. There was an immediate attempt to challenge his ruling and force a debate by moving that he quit the chair. But the delegates voted this down. Many of them, it appeared, were unhappy about the pensions situation but felt they should uphold the president's authority and also defy stubbornly the vitriolic Press comments about their action.

The Post Office members walked out, almost en bloc, led by a delegate wearing dark glasses and holding a black umbrella. A girl delegate ran to the rostrum to present Len Lever with a wreath. The rest of the delegates stayed put but many of them jeered those departing and there was a vigorous exchange of uncomplimentary sign language. It was a pretty extraordinary scene.

Even so, the odds are that the union executive will bow to a mounting outcry from branches and will eventually refuse to implement the decision once the conference is over. There is talk of holding a membership ballot which would surely overwhelmingly reject the plan.

I drove back from Margate to London in time to catch the second half of a special Parliamentary Labour Party meeting to discuss drawing up a register of Members' outside interests. The real issue was whether the register should be available to the public, or only to the party officers or the Speaker.

It was a poorly attended session. I was among 28 MPs who

backed a public register. There were nine against. Now the Deputy Leader, Ted Short, must take this proposal to the Tories who are sure to veto it. We shall then have to decide whether Labour should go-it-alone, a far more tricky verdict to reach.

10th, Thursday: Relief. In the House this afternoon I heard the news that the CPSA conference had been told by Bill Kendall that the decision about the pensions payout would be reconsidered by the executive and he was confident that the pensioners wouldn't suffer. And the branch delegate from Liverpool, who moved the successful motion, told the conference that there had now been heart-searching in his branch and he would now recommend to the branch that its own proposal should not be implemented. That ought to end that unfortunate episode.

Tony Wedgwood Benn is the centre of another row. This time it is over the implication in a statement by him earlier this week that Rolls-Royce Motors would be nationalised by a Labour Government without compensation. Shares in the firm are on public offer and there are strong suggestions that Tony's remarks deterred some would-be purchasers. He certainly upset some other Shadow Cabinet members although there is considerable dispute over just what he did mean.

Whatever the outcome it didn't deter him from advancing further controversial ideas at our special Communications Group session tonight. My own view was that the Group's thinking now needs pulling together in a document which could form the basis of a Green Paper on the media, with a range of suggestions for reform, which could be issued by the Party Executive to provoke a much wider debate. It was a view which proved generally acceptable.

11th, Friday: One of the two computer schools dealt with specifically in the *Sunday Times* article wrote to me to say that it has issued a Writ against the newspaper and offering to discuss any complaints with me. I had suggested that since they were taking legal action it would be preferable if they put their case to me in writing. Today I received their further letter with what seemed fairly plausible explanations. I shall certainly refer to this letter if the Speaker provides me with Parliamentary time. But my overall anxieties are not dispelled. I wrote today to the Speaker asking for an adjournment debate on the subject.

14th, Monday: The return of capital punishment really is a non-issue now or, as someone quipped in the Commons tearoom, a dead issue. The death penalty for murder in Northern Ireland was effectively abolished tonight in a free vote by 253–94. The 159 majority was slightly bigger than last month's majority against the restoration of capital punishment in Britain for certain categories of murder.

15th, Tuesday: I toured the Ford car plant at Dagenham today. It's not surprising that the EEC is pressing for an end to assembly line production. There's not much dignity of labour about the bulk of the work done here and it's small wonder that men sometimes relieve their feelings with a work stoppage. I'm sure I would.

I got back from Dagenham too late for Question Time. But I quickly learned that the Lonrho affair surfaced in the Commons during the afternoon.

Lonrho's boardroom row about who should run the company has spilled over into a series of disquieting court disclosures, especially that Duncan Sandys, the former Conservative Cabinet Minister, was paid heavily for using the expertise he clearly acquired as Colonial and Commonwealth Relations Secretary. Not only was Sandys to be paid huge sums of money as compensation for giving up consultant's fees from the company when he took over as a highly-salaried chairman but arrangements were made for tax avoidance by making payment in the Cayman Islands, a recognised tax haven.

Heath, in reply to a question, said of the Lonrho case: 'It is the unpleasant and unacceptable face of capitalism but one should not suggest the whole of British industry consists of practices of this kind.'

His reference to capitalism, to which he is so dedicated, was a bit rich. But the revelations are obviously causing grave concern among Ministers, coming just as the Government is defending its pay limit of £1 a week plus 4 per cent for rises.

Sandys is a political has-been. There is no suggestion of illegality involving him. But the case finishes his Parliamentary credibility.

I voted for an Opposition censure motion on the Government for 'gross mishandling' of the Rolls-Royce situation since the firm's bankruptcy in 1971. The debate turned into a bit of a wrangle between Government supporters and Tony Wedgwood Benn over what he was supposed to have said about nationalisation without compensation. He contended that the Tories placed a construction upon his words that was unjustified. The Tories were able to point to the confusion which had led the Shadow Cabinet to make a statement, explaining away what he did.

Once that vote was over I went to Islington for the annual Mayor-making and returned to the House in good time for a late vote on the inadequacy of the Government's allowance for school building costs.

16th, Wednesday: A dozen Labour MPs with varying degrees of interest in broadcasting lunched with BBC chairman Sir Michael Swann at Broadcasting House. The discussion ranged over violence and pornography on TV, balance and bias, and took in BBC structure and finance. Swann, new to the job, will not sever his links with Edinburgh University until the autumn and will remain a part-time chairman until then. It enabled him to parry the really sticky questions by insisting he needs more time to sort things out – a fair enough reaction.

Back at the Commons I tried a quick check to see whether Lonrho had contributed to Tory Party funds since the Labour Government's 1967 Companies Act made it necessary for these handouts to be publicly declared. But I drew a blank.

Still, I told my local Party management committee tonight that the Lonrho affair not only made it essential to reform company law to ensure a far more comprehensive disclosure of information but also made the case for a public register of MPs' private interests overwhelming.

I also distributed to the delegates a document I drafted in the aftermath of the GLC election to try and stimulate more interest

in improving our Party organisation. I don't like intervening overmuch in this field. We have a full-time agent, John Braggins,
who covers my constituency and that of my MP neighbour,
George Cunningham. But the next time we go to the polls is
likely to be for the General Election and, as I pointed out to the
committee, my interest in that is very direct.

18th, Friday: I was among a small group of Labour MPs and
Labour prospective Parliamentary candidates travelling to Brussels
and on to Cologne for discussions on the Common Market. It
meant getting up at 4.30 a.m. to get an early morning flight to
Brussels and by 9.45 a.m. we were round the table in a Brussels
conference room at the headquarters of the UK Permanent Representative and Ambassador, Sir Michael Palliser.

Palliser was away but his deputy, Bob Goldsmith, the Minister,
with a bevy of senior British diplomats, conferred with us. We
went on to spend the rest of the day at the EEC's Berlaymont
headquarters, meeting a gaggle of officials, including Commission
Vice President Simonet, to range over regional policy, prices and
the Common Agricultural Policy, social policy, economic and
monetary policy and energy policy.

We went by train to Cologne in the evening and stayed at the
Gustav-Stresemann Institute, apparently a higher education
organisation which receives a State grant and seems to specialise
in bringing together politicians and trades unionists. The Institute
was situated in a magnificent country house, leased from one of
West Germany's big industrialists.

19th, Saturday: The talking began too darned early – at 8.30
a.m., initially in a session with a West German Social Democrat
MP who took a bit of stick from our group, especially for what
most of us thought was a harsh attitude towards Germany's
migrant workers who are not allowed to bring in their families
to live with them.

There was a further morning session on regional policy with a
senior civil servant who was also a Social Democratic Party
member.

The afternoon brought in a speaker from the DGB – the West

German TUC – to discuss worker participation. He was unable to speak in English and the combination of headphones with simultaneous translation, a warm room and a legacy of tiredness from Friday morning's early start, proved too much. I dozed off and was not alone. I came round in time to play a full part in the subsequent question and answer spell and to explain the approach of the British trade unions.

20th, Sunday: Before we returned home from Dusseldorf, we had time for a very enjoyable boat trip down the Rhine from Bonn.

Among our conclusions: that all the Socialists and Social Democrats we met remain baffled by the British Labour Party boycott of the European Parliament and some of them bitterly resent it; that the Europeans have failed to grasp adequately the utter dismay of the British people at the soaring cost of living which they blame very largely on to Market entry; that there is still a long way to go before we can be sure that regional policy will be of worthwhile benefit to us.

The three MPs in the group – Jim Bennett, Tom Cox and myself – all agreed on one thing: that the seven Parliamentary candidates were excellent future material for the Parliamentary Labour Party. True, one of them showed an undue interest in whether he would have time to nip home for tea from the Commons if he was elected. But he was rapidly disillusioned.

21st, Monday: Just a couple of brief and not very meaningful interventions from the Front Bench for me during Post Office questions related to broadcasting. But all the interest was centred on a surprise statement to be made by the Chancellor, Anthony Barber, about public expenditure. No one expected he would increase it !

The customarily gloomy face of Enoch Powell looked positively gleeful when Barber got up to announce the kind of cuts which Powell consistently demands. They added up to £500 million worth in the next financial year and £100 million this year.

The main cutbacks were on roads, the nationalised industries and certain local authority spending. Denis Healey, for us, called it 'very grave' and Barber's attempts to play down the inevitable impact were none too convincing. We are sure to want a debate immediately after the two week Bank Holiday recess which starts at the end of this week.

Yet in the tearoom there was far more interest being shown among Labour Members over the future of Jim Callaghan, the Shadow Foreign Secretary and former Labour Chancellor. All the week-end Press speculation has suggested he is front-runner to become top man at the International Monetary Fund.

His departure from the Westminster scene, which seems certain if the offer is confirmed, would not only mean a Front Bench reshuffle of some kind. Jim's position as a pillar of the non-intellectual Right in the Party means that if he goes it is bound to disturb the political balance, not so much in the Shadow Cabinet, but on the Party's National Executive where he sits as treasurer and is also vice-chairman this year.

22nd, Tuesday: I have run into difficulty over securing an adjournment debate on computer training schools. The Principal Clerk to the Table Office, which deals with matters of this kind, wrote to me to say that the Speaker's Office was in touch with him about my application. But he pointed out that I can't discuss on the adjournment anything for which the Government has no administrative responsibility.

That certainly applies to a good part of my case – indeed, I really want legislation to give the Government full responsibility. Rather than opt for a restricted and inadequate debate I shall try another method. I may go for a Ten Minute Rule Bill, a way of bringing in Private Member's legislation.

It means I would get 10 minutes to make a speech at peak Commons 'listening time', immediately after Question Time in the afternoon. There is little chance of actually achieving legislative change by his method, especially at this late stage of a Parliament when the timetable is crammed. But the issue would be well spotlighted.

The days for Ten Minute Rule Bills are limited in number and usually much sought after. I checked with the Public Bill Office and found there is nothing more than I can do about trying to bag a day until after the coming recess. An alternative would be to table a series of questions to Ministers which might draw even more attention to the problem.

A Ministerial resignation was announced. Lord Lambton, Under-Secretary for the RAF, has quit for 'personal and health reasons', according to his statement. Lambton has been wrangling in the Commons to retain the courtesy title of 'Viscount Lambton' even though he decided to renounce the earldom of Durham on the death of his father. But the gossip was that there could be more in this resignation than meets the eye. There was an extraordinary amount of Ministerial activity around the House tonight.

23rd, Wednesday: This morning's newspapers carried the Lambton story fully. They also ran reports about an international vice scandal involving a 'top British diplomat' who is a member of the aristocracy. This tale originated in the German magazine Stern and followed a recent *News of the World* report of 'a top people's sex ring'.

It looked very much as though a link between Lambton and this scandal stuff was being hinted at. By the time I reached Westminster the confirmation was in the London evening newspaper headlines. Lambton had made a further statement, admitting a 'sordid story' involving 'a casual acquaintance with a call girl and one or two of her friends'.

So the lid was off. Heath is to make a Commons statement tomorrow. And there is a strong suggestion that at least one more Minister is involved, probably more senior than Lambton. The tearoom was rife with rumour and name-dropping.

Tonight I went to the Independent Broadcasting Authority headquarters in Brompton Road where London area MPs had an informal cocktail party with IBA Board members and senior officers and some of the top brass of the Thames, London Weekend and Southern TV companies. I got back to the House in time to intervene during the Employment and Training Bill debate. I sought Government assurances about staff conditions at the proposed Manpower Services Commission, a matter worrying the Civil and Public Services Association which represents the bulk of the staff to be transferred from the Department of Employment. The Minister of State, Robin Chichester-Clark, gave me a general assurance but said he could not do so in 'the broad terms' I wanted, whatever that meant.

24th, Thursday: It's turned into quite a Parliamentary week. The Lambton affair is understandably filling the newspapers and will doubtless continue to do so. Lambton has issued yet another statement, this time declaring his innocence of charges being brought against him under the Dangerous Drugs Act.

I went to lunch at the IBA with the chairman, Lord Aylestone, and his Board. By the time I got back to Westminster, Lord Jellicoe, the Lord Privy Seal and Leader of the Lords, had also quit the Government, Jellicoe, like Lambton, admitted involvement with prostitutes. Again like Lambton, he asserted that there was no question of blackmail or any security risk.

The Chamber was packed for Heath's statement. He was heard in silence. He said that as far as he knew there were no grounds to suppose that any other Minister or member of the public service was involved. It was a carefully qualified rebuttal of more scandal to come. Heath was satisfied too, that security was not endangered. But again there was a qualification. He would ask the Security Commission, headed by a Judge, Lord Diplock to report to him direct after looking into this aspect, just to be sure.

It was low key stuff, inevitably. So was Harold Wilson's response. He had a private session with Heath before the Prime Minister's statement. But he assured the House that there would be no 'carve-up'. Certainly, it was essential that Harold and the Labour Party generally should avoid seeking to make any political capital out of this Government misfortune. Not that we need to.

Several Backbenchers rose to let Heath know of their sympathy, to offer their condolences to the erring ex-Ministers whose political careers have been shattered and even to congratulate Heath for his handling of the whole incredible episode. Only Leo Abse, the diminutive Welsh Labour lawyer-MP, reminded Heath that he too had a responsibility which could not be shrugged off since he picked his own Ministerial team.

Outside the Chamber though, quite a few Labour Members took the view that all this sympathy had gone a bit too far, that it smacked unduly of the establishment old pals' act with MPs rallying around rather too readily to protect their own which was justified criticism. It had all got rather overdone. There is little support for Jim Wellbeloved, the Labour MP for Erith, who has made the most fuss about Lambton and the implications. But a balance is needed. I tried to reflect this in a BBC radio interview. I said no one should be sanctimonious or holier-than-thou but there was a serious issue of public confidence involved.

Despite Heath's statement, rumours continued to sweep Westminster. I have now heard the names of four other Ministers mentioned as possible candidates for the blacklist. Everyone seems certain that a Duke is also concerned. There is no way of telling whether there is real substance in these further suggestions. But I shall be surprised if the Sunday papers don't add to our knowledge.

I know nothing of Lambton and from what I have read and heard of him, can't say I warm to him. George Jellicoe, however, was responsible for the Civil Service and we met at last year's CPSA conference where we were both guest speakers. I had a very pleasant dinner with him and his wife, Philippa, and the union leadership. He seemed a most likeable type and got on well with the union people, although I have noticed before how curiously impressed many union men are by a title. It helped him in this relationship. What I did feel was that Jellicoe was remarkably naïve politically for a man holding Cabinet rank. His naïvety seems to have stretched beyond politics.

31st, Thursday: With the House in recess for two weeks, I spent a few days away touring Derbyshire with the family. I got back to London today to catch up in more detail on the news I had only heard in snatches. The Lambton scandal has dragged on and third and fourth Ministers have been publicly cleared by Heath in a statement, without being named. His statement follows a *Sunday People* story in which Norma Levy, the woman who brought Lambton into disrepute, alleged further Ministerial indiscretions.

There are now some sweeping suggestions of cheque book journalism and also that compromising peephole photographs of Lambton at the Levy flat were taken by newspapermen. It looks as though Fleet Street's role in all this is becoming decidedly questionable.

Far more important than this scandal, however, is yesterday's decision by the Labour Party National Executive Committee to go ahead with a commitment to nationalise 25 of Britain's largest companies. It had been expected that this specific numerical reference would be dropped from the updated document outlining our future programme under a Labour Government.

The Shadow Cabinet appears to be against the plan and it seems that Harold Wilson made it clear at the meeting of the Executive Committee that when the actual election manifesto is drafted the proposal is a non-runner. He sees it as an electoral liability. But Tony Benn and Judith Hart, two Shadow Ministers who sit on the Executive, opposed his view and won on a 7–6 vote – which means that the bulk of the Executive were abstainers or absentees.

I can't see any sense in playing a numbers game over this. Michael Foot, MP, was apparently among those out-voted. He is the best known and most respected Leftwinger in the leadership so it is not a simple Left versus Right issue. No doubt the Tories, well supported by the Press, will make the most of this one.

June

1st, Friday: Harold Wilson has issued a remarkably blunt statement in which he declares that he anticipates that the Shadow Cabinet, which has joint responsibility for the Party's election manifesto with the National Executive Committee, will 'not hesitate to use its veto at the appropriate time' to kill off the 25 companies scheme as part of our next General Election platform.

It is his most forthright assertion of leadership for a long time and will certainly command overwhelming support within the Parliamentary Labour Party. But there is sure to be a stiff fight back by Leftwingers on the old much-argued issue of who runs the Party – the Parliamentary leadership or the Party conference? Use of the word 'veto' is sure to prove provocative.

The whole episode leaves me feeling uneasy. It is letting the Tories right off the hook. They are in deep difficulty over Lonrho and that unacceptable face of their own capitalism, over the Lambton-Jellicoe mess, and still very much over prices. Now the Press have an excellent alternative stick with which to beat the Labour Party, something most of them will grasp with pleasure. Especially so, since none of the daily newspapers will give us any worthwhile support on public ownership. Attention will inevitably be effectively diverted from the Tory troubles to ours, even though ours may be the result of perfectly genuine and legitimate democratic argument.

I am no recent convert to the idea of a major extension of public ownership. But we seem to have adopted a curious approach. If we really want to tackle the commanding economic heights, then banking and insurance are far more crucial than manufacturing industry. Yet before completing the Party's inquiries into the financial institutions – the area of economic management which probably requires priority political treatment

– we have rushed ahead with these other proposals in undue detail. Our emphasis may well turn out to be misplaced in both tactical and policy-making terms.

'Surgery' tonight was mostly a succession of housing cases. There was also an Irishman with a hard luck story. He said he was broke and asked where I could send him to raise his fare so that he could get to an East London emergency social security office in the morning to collect a special payment. There's nowhere to send this sort of case on a Friday night. I 'loaned' him a few bob and will be astonished if I see it again.

2nd, Saturday: A couple of Sunday newspapers were on to me late tonight for comments as Opposition spokesman on Press matters. They wanted my reaction to *News of the World* and *Sunday People* denials of any impropriety in their respective behaviour in dealing with the Lambton case. I repeated quite fully a short statement I put out to the Press Association yesterday in which I stressed my support for genuine investigative reporting but not for muck-raking. I also expressed surprise at the silence of the Press Council, the newspaper industry's self-proclaimed guardian of journalistic ethics and standards.

4th, Monday: Those few days away from home last week meant the postbag was bulging. I dictated some 40 letters this morning to Doreen Wright who in addition to part-time secretarial work for me does a great deal of voluntary work for her local Labour Party.

Tonight it was announced that the Press Council will hold its own probe into the way the newspapers handled the Lambton affair. A Tory MP made a formal complaint to the Council but I have been on both BBC television and radio over the weekend, as well as featuring in newspaper reports, knocking the Council for staying on the sidelines so I suppose I can claim a bit of credit for the change of attitude.

5th, Tuesday: I lunched at Admiralty House today as the guest of Kenneth Baker, the Parliamentary Secretary to the Civil Service

Department. The lunch was in honour of Senator Renzo Forma, Italy's Minister for Bureaucratic Reform (a decidely odd title) and a member of the Italian Cabinet. The other guests included Sir William Armstrong, permanent Head of the Civil Service, and not one of Whitehall's more endearing figures. His approach certainly upset the unions in the recent Civil Service pay dispute.

The venue took me back up memory lane. My last visit to Admiralty House was as a young Fleet Street reporter when the Whitehall building caught fire in the early hours of the morning. That was around 18 years ago.

8th, Friday: The morning papers didn't much like Labour's up-dated 'Programme for Britain', described by Harold Wilson at its Transport House launching yesterday as 'socially relevant and radically progressive'. The row about the 25 companies has taken the edge off it somewhat, and sadly so because it certainly is a radical document. I would say it is undoubtedly Leftwing in emphasis by past Party standards. And it is massive enough in its scope to provide enough work to last the next two or three Labour governments. *The Times* seemed sure it would lose us the next election. Which makes it surprising that the newspaper hasn't welcomed it warmly.

Enoch Powell made a speech at Stockport implying that Tory anti-Common Market voters should not support the Government at the election. He said the country has a right to vote on Britain's entry to the EEC and harped lengthily on the theme of national sovereignty. He appeared to be saying 'Vote Labour'. His kind of support we can certainly do without.

There is hardly a major policy issue left on which he backs his own Government. Yet he apparently has no intention of resigning the Tory Whip in the Commons. As always, he chose his words with meticulous care. His speeches are usually clouded with ambiguity at key points. It's a significant comment on his sense of values that he can blandly advise others to pack in support for the Tories yet refuses to accept the consequences of his own brand of logic and do the same thing himself, formally, by quitting.

Powell's style of delivery is usually far more formidable than his detailed argument. There are very few MPs for whom the

House bars and tearoom empty when their names flash up on the annunciator to indicate that they are speaking in the Chamber. It probably comes down to Heath and Wilson, primarily because of their positions and the potential importance of their remarks, and Michael Foot and Powell, primarily for the force of their oratory. Roy Jenkins should perhaps be included since he became a Backbench 'rebel'.

11th, Monday: The House resumed with a debate on Northern Region affairs which Christopher Chataway, winding up for the Government, sought to use to stir the Labour Party public owner-ship troubles. It was an ineffective effort, though.

12th, Tuesday: I wanted to get from Westminster to Marble Arch by car and set out just after midday. It should have given me plenty of time to keep a 12.30 appointment. I had reckoned without the State visit of Nigeria's General Gowon; streets were closed, traffic diverted, great and glorious traffic jams everywhere. It's ridiculous to encourage this in the middle of the working day. I shall put down a couple of Parliamentary questions to Robert Carr, the Home Secretary, to draw attention to the situa-tion and try to prevent a repeat. Inconvenience apart, it must be a dreadfully costly business for industry and commerce. Londoners suffer enough from traffic chaos by sheer accident without having it thrust upon them by design.

We had whipped votes on the Bill to reorganise the National Health Service's administration. But the Whip was off for the important issue of whether free family planning services should be allowed to continue. Islington's Labour Council has intro-duced this service and I have previously spoken in the House in favour of it. But the reorganisation means it ceases to be a borough responsibility and the Government wants the new area health authorities to end it. There are a number of Labour MPs, mostly Catholic apparently, who take a similar view – hence the lack of a Whip. The Tories took a different disciplinary line and kept their Whip on, however.

We could hardly hope to win in those circumstances, even though we anticipated that a few Tories might rebel. The debate dragged on well beyond midnight and quite a few of our MPs went home. But a fair number of us stuck it out to record our votes and ensure that the outcome didn't look too one-sided when the heads were counted.

13th, Wednesday: This morning I showed a women's club from my constituency around Parliament. I'm a poor Parliamentary historian and consequently a somewhat inadequate guide. I usually manage to learn something from my charges on these occasions. Nevertheless, they enjoyed their visit immensely. I think the real highlight for most of them was not so much the ornate splendour of the Lords or the restrained dignity of the Commons Chamber but a simple stroll on the Terrace.

The House debated the Government's proposal for a new airport at Maplin. The Government squeezed home by nine votes, despite a rebellion by a small group of determined Tories. But only after losing an important amendment on which a bigger group of Tories either voted with us or abstained. It should cause second thoughts about the whole wildly expensive project and the strength of Commons feeling against it is bound to achieve some Ministerial anxiety.

Tony Crosland has had longstanding objections to Maplin and finally persuaded the Parliamentary Labour Party to back his stand. It enabled him to put up a confident Front Bench performance for us which contrasted sharply with the hesitant showing of Eldon Griffiths, the Tory Ministerial spokesman.

14th, Thursday: Members of the Parliamentary Labour Party's Economic and Finance Group really got to grips with capitalism – we visited the Stock Exchange. It was interesting to exchange views with members of the Stock Exchange Council but it's certainly not my scene. The milling crowd of brokers and jobbers and those outdated toppers, made it all seem like Derby Day at Epsom. And the results are not so dissimilar either.

Tonight's Parliamentary Labour Party meeting brought a forceful speech from Sid Bidwell, Southall's MP. He dealt with a House of Lords' decision earlier in the week that the 1971

Immigration Act should operate retrospectively and thus put at risk many illegal immigrants whose length of stay in Britain had been thought to give them immunity from prosecution under existing laws.

Sid is dedicated to fostering improved race relations and has a large immigrant community in his own constituency so he can talk from firsthand experience. He pleaded for full Party support for an amnesty for these people. Shadow Home Secretary Shirley Williams has already given public backing to this suggestion and the Shadow Cabinet is now to consider the situation. It will be surprising, and disturbing, if it fails to go along with this.

16th, Saturday: We went to Tonbridge, Kent, tonight where Pat and I were the main guests of the local Labour Party at a social evening. I made a brief speech in which I contended that the Tories would make the next General Election 'one of the dirtiest and most expensive campaigns of desperate distortion ever'. I quoted the £500,000 to be spent by the anti-nationalisation outfit, Aims of Industry, as an example.

It is often the case that Labour parties which are based in the heart of what is generally regarded as strong Tory territory, have plenty of heart and energy. Tonbridge struck me as an excellent example.

19th, Tuesday: This afternoon Reg Prentice and I had a meeting with leaders of the Printing and Kindred Trades Federation, the joint body which represents printing unions. They were particularly concerned at what they regarded as misguided Commons statements in the past, particularly from John Davies when he was Secretary for Trade and Industry, about overmanning in the industry.

My brother, Ken, and his wife, Nora, are visiting us from Australia where they have been living for the past 17 years. I showed them around the House and got them tickets for the Strangers' Gallery this evening. They didn't find it easy to make out what was going on. Nor did I. It was the Local Government (Scotland) Bill. It's not for those of us from south of the border – except when the votes come.

20th, Wednesday: Dennis Skinner, the Bolsover blunderbuss, is one of the most active and certainly the most aggressive of the 1970 intake of Members. He doesn't always endear himself to his colleagues on our Benches but the Tories positively bristle whenever he gets to his feet in the Chamber.

He clobbered them today. Paul Channon, the bright and youthful Housing Minister, was on the receiving end. He had to admit that house prices have almost doubled since the Tories took office and looked suitably shamefaced.

Dennis blamed the Housing Finance Act and when the Tories shouted 'Nonsense' at him he suggested some of them were upset because they had probably been lining their pockets out of it. Just to rub it in, he added: 'Is it any wonder that the property spivs and now even prostitutes, are competing with each other in declaring that life is better under the Conservatives'.

The Shadow Cabinet had a long session and there were rumours going around later that Michael Foot had taken a critical view of Tony Benn's tactics in the dispute over the 25 companies proposal in the Party programme. I heard that Harold Wilson was not spared from some criticism either, over his 'veto' statement and there could be another stormy session when the National Executive Committee meets again next week. This issue is taking a long time to fade away. Indeed, it seems it will nag on right up to Party conference in October. Just the kind of running battle in our own ranks that Heath needs.

Tonight I called briefly on a crippled constituent with a problem, then looked in at the Islington Central Labour Party's monthly management committee meeting. I gave them a quick rundown on recent Parliamentary happenings and added an attack on the 'unacceptable face of Toryism'. Rather to my surprise, I got no questions on our public ownership row but that was probably because of resolutions on the agenda on this which were due to be discussed later in the evening.

21st, Thursday: One of my Canonbury Ward councillors, Vic Cordwell, a stalwart for the council tenants in the area, died recently and a by-election is under way. I put in a couple of hours canvassing tonight while the House debated Northern Ireland once again.

The doorstep reception was generally very good. Most people seemed pleased to see their MP and I increasingly find that I am recognised on these occasions without introducing myself. That's not just good for the ego. It should be reflected in my vote at the next General Election.

It wouldn't be sensible to set too much store by the handshakes on a canvass but it does seem to indicate that politicians are not really in the public disrepute which is sometimes rather too glibly suggested by outside commentators and some of our own number. There's always an exception, of course. One awkward customer said: 'I never vote. I'm not going to until they get me a house and get rid of the nig-nogs.'

22nd, Friday: Two women came to see me at the 'surgery' about their grim living conditions. Damp, collapsed ceilings, rats. I have visited this house in the past and the public health officials have been active but the landlord is impossible. He does the minimum necessary, takes as long as possible to do it and has no concern whatsoever for the tenants. I shall ask the Housing Manager to consider recommending a closure order on the Property. It seems to be the only sensible step to take.

23rd, Saturday: Ted Short, our Deputy Leader, has been making a speech today warning of a possible autumn General Election. There's been a renewed outburst of speculation on this lately, both in the Press and among MPs.

The semblance of an economic boom with rising output, falling unemployment and a fair measure of industrial peace, account for the feeling. Delay, it is argued, could find the Government in the throes of a fresh pay explosion, still bigger price rises and a balance of payments crisis. Meanwhile the opinion polls mostly provide a fillip for the Tories, showing the two main parties uncomfortably close which must look healthy to any Government after three years of contentious office.

Even so, I doubt that autumn forecast will come up. It's an enormous gamble for Heath to take. Above all, price rises could still see him come a cropper. He still has nearly two years to go.

He and his colleagues are fond of their power. Why should they risk tossing it away so soon?

Much as I would like an early election – after all, despite those polls, the local government results must make us favourites to win – I don't reckon the Party is yet in adequate battle order. All the more reason therefore, for Ted Short to alert the troops. Just in case.

An autumn election could bring me a spot of personal inconvenience. I am due to visit America in September and would have to get back to my constituency fast. Moreover Harold Wilson has let me know that he will want me around at the time.

25th, Monday: A row broke out last week over charges by Campaign, the advertising trade journal, and Social Audit, the new consumer magazine, that commercial television companies are abusing the Independent Broadcasting Authority's rules that advertising shouldn't exceed a daily average of six minutes an hour and should normally be limited to seven minutes in any one hour. A series of spot checks at the week-end by the *Sunday Times* seemed to substantiate these findings.

I tabled a question quickly to Sir John Eden, the Posts and Telecommunications Minister, when the suggestions were made and pursued it with him from the Front Bench today. I referred to serious allegations that thousands of pounds may have been illicitly made by the programme companies and asked if he was satisfied that the IBA is satisfactorily carrying out its statutory duties. I said he should have urgent talks with the IBA and should press for regular publication of all the relevant data and statistics about TV advertising so that misunderstandings – if that is what happened in this case – should not arise in future.

Eden said the IBA was urgently investigating and that, although he was concerned, it was firstly a matter for the Authority. The IBA claims the allegations are based on inaccurate figures but the denials have not been convincing so far and it may be necessary to return to the issue.

This evening I kept a date to speak to the London area committee of the Civil and Public Services Association. My impression was that those at the meeting were mostly members of a

Left-wing union 'ginger group' and included a number of International Socialists. Since I had opted to speak about the need for an incomes policy under a Labour Government, I expected a rough ride. In the event, it was a remarkably friendly session with a good deal of divergent opinion.

It meant I missed a good deal of the debate about the proposed new Parliamentary building. I still remain decidedly unhappy at the projected size and cost of this venture.

The MP lobbyists for the building have been active. They argue that Spence and Webster, the architects, won a contest set up by the House and say that a vote against this building is tantamount to a vote against any new building. The House will not go through all this again for decades, they forecast.

It's a persuasive line. It could well turn out to be the case. But I still feel we have our priorities wrong. In the event, though not without continued misgivings, I voted for a new building 'in due course' – the Government line which meant acceptance of the principle. That motion was carried by 292 votes to 68 – a surprisingly high turnout of MPs since everyone had a free vote. But I opposed the further proposal for the specific Spence-Webster design. This time the vote for approval was narrowed to 208 against 144. Quite a few MPs obviously decided to register the same doubts as I did.

26th, Tuesday: The Opposition took one of those stands on principle which tend to be all too rare on delicate issues like immigration where electors may easily be alienated.

We tried to gain a safeguard for illegal immigrants to prevent their deportation under the retrospective powers of the 1971 Immigration Act. We asked for an amnesty for those who came here illegally but were settled for six months or more before the Act receives the Royal Assent. Not much to seek for people who are mostly victims of circumstance rather than criminals. It was certainly not a plea for an 'open door' policy. Mrs Shirley Williams, from our Front Bench, stressed that many of these people will live in fear of deportation and will be open to blackmail. Immigrants involved in only minor offences might be questioned about their immigrant status and race relations could be damaged.

Robert Carr, the Home Secretary, contended that everything possible should be done to 'bring to an end this loathsome trade in illegal immigrants'. That, as he knew, was not the point of the argument or cause for dissent. Anyway, he insisted that no new methods of detection are to be used and that people could not be treated as ordinarily resident if they are here in breach of the law. The Tories went on to defeat our proposal by a majority of 39 – to their discredit.

27th, Wednesday: The Liberals got their come-uppance in the House today. John Pardoe is the Liberal Member for North Cornwall. He has appeared unduly anxious to capitalise on the discomfort of both Tory and Labour Parties over the apparent links which some of those in their ranks had in the unsavoury Poulson case.

Of course, there's a nasty smell about it. But Pardoe's nose has turned up too far. Other MPs are convinced he has been using the issue as part of the stop-at-nothing electioneering tactics the Liberals are indulging in to boost their temporary revival. Just as every little local grievance from uneven paving stones to over-flowing dustbins is exploited by them unscrupulously.

Pardoe had a Ten Minute Rule Bill – one more aspect of the Liberal propaganda campaign. This one called for a national minimum wage and was conveniently introduced on the day of the Manchester Exchange Division Parliamentary by-election which the Liberals have been cocky about capturing from us.

As Pardoe paced solemnly from the Bar of the House with his Bill and bowed to the Speaker, in keeping with custom, Liverpool MP Eric Heffer shouted from our Backbenches: 'Mind the cracked pavements!' It virtually brought the House down.

28th, Thursday: Labour MPs were able to cheer themselves up during Prime Minister's questions with a quip or two about the Manchester Exchange result. We held off the Liberal challenge reasonably well. But the Tories took a hiding. They lost their deposit.

This evening the Canonbury by-election was on in my con-stituency. I went there to spend a couple of hours 'knocking up' for our candidate, Fred Johns. That involves a door-by-door reminder to our supporters who have been previously canvassed urging them not to forget to come out and vote.

It's a safe enough seat for us. A Liberal is running and it could well be a repeat of the Manchester Exchange situation with the Tory a poor third.

I got back to the House in good time for a vote against the Government at the end of a two-day foreign affairs debate.

29th, Friday: The Commons today debated the Franks Report which deals with the need to reform the Official Secrets Act. It is of especial interest to me since it involves communication with the public via the media. But it was dealt with by our Home Office Shadow Ministers.

I doubt if there was a great deal of enthusiasm for letting a journalist-MP loose on this one. I spent so long as a poacher that I must be suspect as a really 'safe' gamekeeper. Indeed, I have a dubious distinction which fits me to speak on it: I was once the subject of a Whitehall leak inquiry following a story I wrote back in my Fleet Street days, quoting a Government document weeks ahead of intended publication. The matter was even raised in the House at the time, much to my amusement.

I would certainly favour going much farther than Franks in lifting the often absurd secrecy surrounding official information. I hope the Party can make some commitment to the public 'right to know', allowing ordinary citizens access to many files and documents in Whitehall and the town halls, rather as they do in Sweden.

Since I was unable to speak about this in the House (I could hardly make use of the Backbenches on an issue where my Front Bench duties clearly have relevance) I ensured that my viewpoint came across by recording it in a newspaper article which appeared this morning.

'Surgery' was the usual mixed bag. Several couples seeking new homes, complaints about the Council's housing maintenance service and about a breakdown in laundry facilities in a tower block, a pensioner's problem over Post War Credits and a wrangle between neighbours over noise.

But the most distressing case was that of a young couple, unmarried, the teenage girl carrying their baby in her arms. Neither of their families really had room for them and the girl apparently expected to be turned out of her home soon. Landlords wouldn't look at them because of the child and the Council will only put them on the waiting list, though the youngsters assured me they want to marry.

What a way to start off in life. The boy was earning £26 a week as a plumber. No chance of a mortgage on that income. I put them in touch with a couple of housing associations and ensured that they contacted the Social Services Department in case of any drastic emergency. It's a grim outlook.

We won that Canonbury by-election easily. The Liberals came a poor second and the Tories were trounced into third place. It's another cheerful indicator for me for the next General Election whenever it comes.

July

2nd, *Monday:* The Labour movement has long dragged its feet over industrial democracy. I have talked about the possibilities in recent years informally with a whole range of interested people like Harold Wilson and Reg Prentice, on our political wing, and Jack Jones and David Basnett, respectively the top men in the Transport and General Workers' Union and the General and Municipal Workers' Union and the one thing that does emerge is that there are no easy answers.

I think we should have paid far more attention to the quest for a workable system. Heath is now paying lip service to the need for worker participation and the Liberals have pretensions to a policy.

But the initiative should come from the people most affected – from the unions and their members. At long last – undoubtedly spurred on by the requirement to react to Common Market proposals – the TUC has pronounced. It published plans today for trades unionists to be elected by workers to occupy half the seats on supervisory boards of all companies employing more than 200 people. This goes much farther than the draft directive which the European Economic Community has advanced for worker representation on boards where more than 500 are employed. There are other major differences in the TUC scheme which puts more emphasis on worker interests.

The employers will seek to wreck it. The Government will back away from this kind of attack on managerial prerogative and intrusion on the cosy confines of the boardroom.

It will be a matter of major contention within the Labour Party too. We have to strike an attitude. There are those who believe that the conflict between the two sides of industry – management and managed – must never be blurred. There are also those who feel that 50 per cent worker participation in management is tantamount to the revolution.

The Party should not be too timid. It should give broad support to the TUC plan although it would need to examine some of the fine print very carefully. The TUC is not suggesting that it has published a rigid and final viewpoint. Indeed, the TUC conference in September has yet to discuss the document.

The House debated the pending French nuclear tests and the Government defeated an Opposition motion complaining that Britain failed to protest adequately to France.

Tam Dalyell, West Lothian's MP, has been the most persistent Backbench questioner on this and was sensibly promoted to the Front Bench for the occasion. There was no doubt that he bested Julian Amery, now Minister of State at the Foreign and Commonwealth Office and as bumbling as he was as Housing Minister. The narrow Government majority of ten – 276 votes to 266 – said a lot for the lack of Tory faith in their own performance.

The House of Lords had reversed the Commons decision over free contraception and we had another late night debate in which the Government sought to restore to its Bill the original position so that prescription charges would be levied. This time we did have a Whip – a two-liner which had caused some ill feeling among some Catholic Labour MPs who declared their intention to defy it. Likewise, some Tory MPs refused to support the Government. The 'rebels' just about cancelled each other out. And the Government got home by 247 votes to 220.

Not everyone on our side was prepared to see this as a matter of conscience – the situation which is generally recognised as permitting abstention or even outright opposition to the Party's Whipped vote. I adhere strongly to the view that conscience can only be decided by the individual Member for himself. If a Member displays it too often he will be seen as a phoney. Most MPs use it exceedingly sparingly and I have yet to feel the need to defy the Whip in my three Parliamentary years. Which doesn't mean I won't some time.

3rd, Tuesday: I dropped the idea of a Ten Minute Rule Bill on computer training schools in favour of submitting a series of Parliamentary questions to Ministers. I drafted five to put in –

three to Education, one to Trade and Industry and one to the Home Office.

I lunched with a couple of senior people from the television programme companies who were disturbed by the TV advertising issue. They were unhappy with the offhand fashion in which the IBA has responded to the allegations about breaches of its rules. I shall be quizzing Sir John Eden again on this and suggested to them that it is very much in their interests to see that the IBA refutes the charges publicly, speedily and in detail – if it really can do so.

The Government is under mounting pressure over increased food prices and Tories know that a Labour onslaught on this is bound to hit them at the next General Election whenever it comes.

The tension is rising even faster than the prices now. Heath ran full tilt into trouble at Question Time. He denied a suggestion that the Common Market Commission instructed Britain not to use food subsidies as an anti-inflation measure and told Harold Wilson that the latest figures for disposable income – the difference between price rises and tax paid against the actual increase in the pay packet – was up more under the Tories than under the last Labour Government. It didn't sound very convincing. Few shoppers would accept it. And it emerged later that even Tory Backbenchers criticised Tony Barber, the Chancellor, at their private meeting. They recognise the political consequences of failure to act on the prices front and the prospect of defeat at the polls is beginning to concentrate their minds wonderfully.

4th, Wednesday: There was an uninspiring Commons debate on the future of the railways. After the vote, I went on to Islington where some 200 people packed the annual meeting of St Martin of Tours House, in my constituency, to hear the guest speaker, Sir Keith Joseph, the Secretary of State for Social Services.

St Martin of Tours House is a Catholic voluntary-run hostel for people down on their luck. They may have come from jail, may be alcoholics or any kind of social misfit. They are encouraged to talk to each other about their problems as part of the attempt at rehabilitation and the project appears to enjoy considerable success. I don't share the religious approach of those behind the scheme. Indeed, I thought the pressure on the Minister over the Abortion Act, during questions to him from the audience, was uncalled for in the circumstances of his visit. Furthermore, I remain disturbed by hearing Sir Keith put undue emphasis on the role of voluntary work in the social services field. I have heard him do this in the past to an extent that is unrealistic and verges on excuse-making for the failure of Government to accept its necessary share of responsibility.

However these reservations do not detract from the valuable community service which voluntary bodies can offer and this one is well deserving of support.

5th, Thursday: The Chancellor, Tony Barber, faced a barrage of hostile Commons questions on prices. He surprised the House by appearing to rule out an increase in family allowances as one answer and it looks as though the Cabinet must have decided against this. Barber said Family Income Supplement was a better way of helping the needy. He brushed off the possibility of across-the-board food subsidies. He argued that the cost would be enormous and the well-to-do as well as the poor would benefit.

None of this augers well for the forthcoming round of talks between the Government, employers and unions about the next phase of Heath's so-called incomes policy. And those Tory Back-benchers will become increasingly restive – especially if the Government has bad results at the pending Parliamentary by-elections at the Isle of Ely and Ripon which are now expected to be held before the summer recess.

The House went on to discuss another dose of Northern Ireland legislation – the Emergency Provisions Bill. Other than those MPs with special responsibility or interest in the tragic Ulster situation, the bulk of the House has become bored with the interminable details of legislative attempts to resolve the seemingly insoluble.

The Opposition is generally supporting the Government against the small group of 'rebels' from its own ranks. And, despite a Two-Line Whip, the vote to give the Bill a Third Reading was a mere 58 to 6. Most MPs had gone home.

Some were presumably 'paired' – the system which allows two

Members, one from each side of the House, to register their joint intention to be away for a vote, thus cancelling out each other's absence. This is usually sanctioned without much fuss by the Whips on a Two-Line vote, providing the numbers don't get out of hand. On a Three Liner, it has to be something of major importance for a 'pair' to be approved, say a necessary Ministerial absence abroad or an Opposition Member attending an important trade union conference. On this occasion, some of our MPs left 'unpaired' once it was certain that Labour would not be forcing a vote against the Government on Third Reading of the Bill.

9th, Monday: The issue of undue secrecy and public accountability is becoming of increased political consequence so when I talked to the Islington Fabian Society tonight on 'The Future of Broadcasting', I referred to unnecessary secrecy by both the Independent Broadcasting Authority and the BBC.

I criticised the IBA over its role in the row about advertising time and its 'offhand dismissal' of a matter of legitimate concern. I shall bring this up again in the House next week. I said the BBC put up a ridiculous barrier about disclosing the number of times politicians appear on their programmes and suggested they feared reaction to their undue use of professional rebels like Enoch Powell 'whose pockets must be bulging with programme fees'.

These, I added, were instances of the disturbing mentality that permeates 'our elitist managerial society'. A rearguard action was being fought against justifiable demands for more public accountability and this action was the antithesis of democratic Socialism. It's a theme worth hammering away on.

I hope that Labour in government will really take to heart the call from Harold Wilson for a more open society. He made that in a speech recently, referring to industry. But we should go much farther than that and apply this thinking to Whitehall, Westminster and the town halls as well as the boardrooms.

As for the BBC, my correspondence with them about politicians' appearances is not getting anywhere fast. They are worried that they would be seriously inconvenienced if the relevant figures were published and their editorial judgment would be questioned. I don't doubt it would be. And why not?

There are some politicians, usually those who are most ready to kick their own Party colleagues in the teeth and who therefore make 'good TV or radio', who get a sizeable second income from this source. The important thing, though, is the exaggerated importance which is thus afforded to their views. There is no doubt that the media plays a key part in building up its 'stars', whether they are politicians, entertainers, or, as is sometimes the case, a mixture of both.

10th, Tuesday: This morning we started the first of two planned meetings of the Parliamentary Labour Party to discuss 'Labour's Programme for Britain' – not so much a programme, more a way of life, but no bad thing.

It was a largely uneventful meeting with the passing exception of a brief challenge by Frank Allaun, MP member of the Party National Executive, to Harold Wilson over the Leader's statement about vetoing the 25 companies proposal for the election manifesto. Even that fell a bit flat, mainly because Harold was out of the room at the time. Bob Mellish raised a pertinent point about housing which several speakers contended should be our top priority. Bob said some local authorities couldn't scrape up enough in rents even to pay off the interest on their housing programmes which could run into millions of pounds. If London Transport could be handed over to the Greater London Council to run, debt-free, why couldn't local authorities have their debts wiped out?

The Chamber was packed this afternoon when Dick Taverne moved the writ for the Berwick-on-Tweed by-election caused by the resignation of Lord Lambton. Taverne was out to buck the traditional system of by-election dates being fixed by the Government of the day in seats they held to suit their convenience. Likewise, the official Opposition has a quid pro quo arrangement for its own vacant seats.

Taverne now has his own so-called Party. So he grabbed the chance to embarrass both Government and, to a lesser extent, the Labour Opposition, too. He stressed that a by-election at Ripon is to be held almost immediately, despite upsetting the family of the Tory MP who died only very recently. He pointed out that Berwick would remain unrepresented for some five months unless the writ is moved before the summer recess. The Liberals, of course, backed him. They never hesitate to seize a quick political advantage.

Taverne got a rough ride from our Backbenches and some Tory MPs also had a go at him. He was reminded that he made no protest at the prevailing situation when he was a Minister in the last Labour Government.

His credentials on this are suspect and his motives even more so. Like those Liberals, he is desperately anxious to keep his name before the public.

Yet he had logic on his side today. My natural inclination was to vote with him. There was no official Party advice. But I decided eventually that it was reasonable to look beyond the immediate issue and consider what lay behind the action of the sponsor of the move and I thought there was a good deal more than the public interest in Taverne's mind. So I reluctantly abstained. But I also felt it couldn't be left at that and considered raising the general principle with the Party in some form.

Taverne picked up 25 supporters, including a sprinkling from our ranks. The Government got 194 votes. But many of our abstentionists, like me, would really have preferred to oppose the Government on this and scupper an all-too-cosy expedient.

The other major incident was an angry scene between Heath and Harold Wilson. Harold was determined to get in a question to the Prime Minister about next week's visit to Britain by Portuguese Prime Minister Dr Caetano. There have been horrific reports of Portuguese troops committing atrocities against African peasants in Mozambique. Harold made nimble use of a question about the French nuclear tests in the Pacific by suggesting that Dr Caetano should be replaced as an official Government guest by New Zealand Prime Minister Norman Kirk who has sought to stop the testing. Heath went visibly red and could be heard to shout angrily above the Labour jeers that Harold had abused Question Time. He flatly refused to entertain the proposal to scrap Caetano's visit. He is in an awkward spot, though. If he did cancel the visit it would imply a major climbdown. Yet confirmation of the alleged massacre could utterly wreck Caetano's stay, already under heavy fire as a misplaced gesture of friendship to a dictator. Labour has decided to boycott all the official events connected with the visit and street demonstrations are planned on a considerable scale.

11th, Wednesday: Today's further instalment of our discussion of the Party programme saw the Parliamentary Party somewhere near its debating best. It was a packed meeting to deal with the most controversial section of the document – that concerning public ownership and the scheme to nationalise 25 companies.

It was a meeting with scarcely a trace of rancour, although John Mendelson took a bit of a sideswipe at Harold Wilson, Denis Healey, and Tony Crosland by implication for rushing out statements repudiating policy proposals which had been democratically reached. Yet only Mrs Judith Hart, who 'mothered' the 25 companies commitment through the Party Executive, defended it vigorously. Leftwingers like John Mendelson, Stan Orme and Ian Mikardo all let it be known that much as they sought an extension of the public sector, they could not enthuse over such a specific plan.

Ian Mikardo usually manages a colourful turn of phrase. He said: 'Capitalism today is a man-eating tiger. You are not going to tame it by stroking its fur, saying "Nice pussy" and giving it a saucer of milk.' Another telling speech was made by Edmund Dell, a former junior Minister. He was especially worried by the likely size of the proposed National Enterprise Board which would take charge of the expanded public sector. His doubts about the mechanics of the takeover plans – not the principle – obviously drew a thoughtful response.

What was most striking though was the all-round acceptance of the need to nationalise, using a wide range of 'tools in the kit', as it was put. Harold Wilson wound up the debate with what I assume was a deliberately low key speech in which he emphasised that his personal reservations concerned a handful of words in a 70,000 word document. He ran into a short sharp challenge as the meeting ended from Eric Heffer over his interpretation of the role of the National Enterprise Board but he insisted that he had not moved out of line with the document.

I had an evening session with my local Party executive committee – a smaller body drawn from the general management committee – so that I could stimulate the first moves in readiness for the General Election: not that it's likely this year but we don't intend to be caught napping. There is preparatory work that can be started now.

12th, Thursday: The Security Commission reported today on the call girl cases which led to Lord Lambton and Lord Jellicoe leaving the Government. Heath announced to the House that he accepts the Commission's findings. Ministers will not have 'positive vetting' by the security services but there will be some tightening up of warning procedures to alert new Ministers to the possible pitfalls. The Commission virtually cleared Jellicoe as a security risk but said that Lambton's drug-taking, as well as his resort to prostitutes, made him 'wide open to blackmail' and involved the more serious risk that he could have revealed secrets while under the influence of cannabis.

The Chamber was very full for Heath's statement but it was a largely uneventful occasion. I think everyone's had enough of this squalid affair now. Although there is still the Press Council inquiry to come into the conduct of newspapers. The Security Commission steered clear of this for the most part.

I'd made up my mind to raise the situation arising from the Berwick-on-Tweed writ tonight when the Parliamentary Party holds its usual Thursday meeting and I warned the Party chairman, Douglas Houghton, that I would do so.

If I made too much fuss it could be interpreted as Taverne stampeding the Party into action. But kicking this matter under the carpet would create a far worse impression in the long run by my reckoning. So I told the Party meeting that I abstained with great uneasiness and knew that many others did likewise. The 'hear, hears' around the room underlined that point for me. I asked the Shadow Cabinet to 'take this on board' and received an assurance from the Chief Whip, Bob Mellish, that this would be done, although he referred to the technical difficulties which can crop up over the timing of by-elections.

There was a surprise defeat for the Government later. It lost by 21 votes over its proposal to continue to allow the export of live animals for slaughter. The Agriculture Minister, Joe Godber, had to come to the Despatch Box to promise that after the implications had been considered there will be a Government statement. There has been a lot of lobbying by the public against this revolting trade and it seems that 23 Tories voted with us to provide Heath with another minor embarrassment.

13th, Friday: 'Surgery' took about an hour and three-quarters and I hurried off to the Islington Town Hall where the local pensioners' Branch was holding its second annual meeting. I found I had been re-elected as honorary president. I was able to congratulate the Branch on achieving nearly 900 members – just about the only thing that had gone up in the past two years faster than prices, I maintained.

It's impossible to make a speech to pensioners without rapping the Government. I attacked Heath for refusing to really safeguard pensioners against the rising cost of living and failing to understand the pensioners' plight. I said the rising cost of Mr Edward Heath was reflected in the pauperism which pensioners still suffer in what the Government Ministers claim is an increasingly affluent society.

There were plenty of questions. These people are understandably bitter that their next rises, due in October, will have been largely swallowed up by price increases before they see the extra cash.

16th, Monday: The Minister of Posts and Telecommunications, Sir John Eden, admitted in the House that advertising rules on television have been broken on 'rare occasions'. He argued, however, that the Independent Broadcasting Authority has adequate controls and has received satisfactory explanations of the breaches. I pressed him further from our Front Bench and later told several interested journalists who phoned me that the reply was 'whitewash'. I said I would write to Eden with details of alleged breaches and ask for a full explanation. I have heard that the IBA and programme companies thought he should have defended them more robustly when I questioned him previously. They could hardly warm to this performance – but it looks as though their case is feeble so he can hardly be blamed.

Question Time ended with one of those silly spots. It in-

volved Commons catering facilities. These are not a Government
responsibility but are a matter for the House itself. Consequently,
they were answered by Dr Reginald Bennett, a Tory Backbencher
who is chairman of the kitchen committee. It was mostly the
prices which worried MPs. Dr Bennett could hardly use Heath's
permanent excuse for increases – worldwide shortages. But he
sounded almost triumphant when he disclosed that a ham sandwich has only gone up by a penny since November and bread
and butter by a mere halfpenny. One Tory critic nonetheless
thought 16p for a ham sandwich unreasonable. 'Is there,' he
asked unhelpfully 'a world shortage of ham sandwiches?' Another
Tory wanted to know why an orange cost 5½p in the Members'
tearoom but 10p in the Members' dining room. Said Dr Bennett,
amid hilarity: 'Because it has to be brought by a waiter.' Someone was unkind enough to suggest that Dr Bennett, who looks
decidedly well fed, never used the tearoom anyway.

It was all a waste of Parliamentary time. But I see no reason
to grudge a few minutes of light relief. It doesn't happen very
often.

A series of meetings occupied me for the rest of the afternoon
and evening while the House debated Scottish affairs. First I saw
two young social workers from Islington about sports and recrea-
tional facilities in the borough; then came a session of London
Labour MPs to discuss making better use of redundant railway
land; and at County Hall I met members of the Party's Regional
Council to discuss public relations.

17th, Tuesday: Harold Wilson led the Opposition attack over the
visit of Portugal's Caetano. Harold has been accused of apply-
ing double standards and some newspapers have been more
anxious to make this charge stick than to pursue the truth of the
massacre allegations. The Tory Backbenchers harassed him but
he took the view that although people with different political
and social systems can search together for peace and understanding when Britain meets the Soviet Union, eastern European
countries or China, it is not as an ally. It was a legitimate
distinction to draw and he underlined the impossibility of justify-
ing 'red carpet' treatment for Portugal in the present situation.

True, he would have been on better ground if the last Labour

Government had adopted a tougher line on Portugal and Greece. Sir Alec Douglas Home made the best of this. But the bull point remained unanswerable: talk and trade are one thing, military alliance with a totalitarian regime is another. And feting its leader is sheer hypocrisy.

Tonight it was the Greater London Council reception at the Festival Hall. I went rather reluctantly to one of these annual occasions while the Tories were in control at County Hall and considered that once was enough. This year's invitation from a Labour GLC chairman, Arthur Wicks, an Islington member of the Council, was far more acceptable.

18th, Wednesday: This morning saw the third and final Parliamentary Labour Party session on the Party programme. It was an anti-climax after last week's public ownership debate and was poorly attended. I would have spoken briefly on the communications section of the document but it was nearly one o'clock before that part was reached, the MPs still there had dwindled to a handful and I didn't bother.

I had hoped to hear the opening speeches by Heath and Harold Wilson on the Opposition's motion censuring the Government for failing to control rising prices. But I had to make several phone calls and deal with a lobby by North London public house tenants who fear they will be thrown out of their pubs by the brewers in favour of managers.

I only heard snatches of the speeches. It seemed though, that Harold was in far better form than yesterday. His best crack was that Heath had broken more female hearts than Casanova did in a lifetime – and at least Casanova's victims were left with memories to console them.

Heath spent a long time arguing about what Labour would do if elected. It provoked the inevitable retorts from our Benches that the Tories are in Government, not us. The Prime Minister's speech was lengthy but the only glimmer of a fresh thought was his announcement that the Government will put forward a proposal for threshold agreements on pay, aimed at linking them to the cost of living index. The idea originally stemmed from the unions. But the Government commitment to it is new.

I moved on to a Fabian Society meeting on industrial relations and left before it ended for the Islington meeting of my local Party management committee where I gave my usual report of the past month's Parliamentary happenings and answered questions.

I was back in the House for the closing speeches in the prices debate which were delivered by Ted Short, the Deputy Leader, for us, and Tony Barber, the Chancellor, for the Tories. There was a rowdy finish with Barber and Harold Wilson shouting at each other across the Despatch Box against a crescendo of Back-bench sound. Our motion was defeated by 314 votes to 288.

19th, Thursday: I drove up to the Fens to give a hand in the Isle of Ely by-election campaign. The poll takes place next week and it seems that Liberal intervention could make it a photo-finish result. My guess is a narrow Tory win but anything could happen in this one.

I know the area well. Pat is from Ely where her parents still live and I once worked on a local newspaper in Wisbech. I can recall reporting a speech by Sir Harry Legge Bourke, the long-serving Tory MP whose death has led to this by-election scrap.

Helpers appeared to be a bit thin on the ground to me although midweek is not a good time for Labour volunteers, who are mostly at work. On the other hand, the Labour posters were plentiful, an encouraging sign. I linked up with Party full-time officials, drafted in to organise, and did a loudspeaker tour of Ely, particularly around the market. In the evening I carried on canvassing.

20th, Friday: Two housing cases at 'surgery' gave me special food for thought. One woman couldn't understand why she was unable to get rehoused through the GLC. She suggested that neighbours who had been successful must have 'greased a palm or two'. A second woman, also seeking a transfer, implied that she would be only too ready to pay for it. These people were under strain. They felt powerless to break through what appeared to them to be a bureacratic wall. But allowing for all that, it does indicate that the continual talk of corruption in national and local government is having an effect. I wonder whether people increasingly believe that politicians and public servants are easily bribed? The rash of headlines, from Watergate to Poulson, make it hard to blame them but its rough on the vast majority of MPs, councillors, civil and public servants, who do an honest job to the best of their ability and usually for limited reward.

A constituent called to see me tonight with a most unusual problem. Her husband is serving an 18-years jail sentence for armed robbery. The woman is aged 30 and has a two-year-old son. She badly wants a second child through artificial insemination with her husband's semen. She has her doctor's support but the Home Office has told him it would only allow this in the most exceptional circumstances. The case has already received some newspaper publicity. So I wasn't surprised by the visit. Enlisting her MP's support is probably this woman's best chance. I suggested to her that the doctor should write to me setting out as fully as possible the medical case and other relevant grounds so that I could put it to the Home Secretary for her.

21st, Saturday: The *Sun* newspaper this morning gave me an editorial pat on the back for a statement I put out yesterday remarking on the 'appalling' judgment earlier in the week of the Law Lords in banning publication of a *Sunday Times* article on thalidomide children on grounds of contempt.

Some Parliamentary comment on this situation cropped up while I was in Ely and I thought I should say something about it in view of my Party responsibility. I pointed out that it was a Government Minister, the Attorney-General, whose appeal was successful and drew attention to a series of instances which 'make a mockery of the Conservative pledge of open government'. Under a Labour Government, I added, there would have been a Fleet Street outcry but criticism of Heath had been remarkably restrained.

I finished with a dig at the Press Council for failing to 'get off its backside' when there was 'Government connivance in creeping encroachment on freedom of speech'.

23rd, Monday: I lunched with a TV programme company man

and it confirmed to me the anxiety felt over the allegations that advertising time limits were flouted.

Our monthly meeting of the Party's Greater London Regional Council had its first progress report from Sir Reg Goodwin since Labour captured the GLC. The most ominous aspect, with clear Parliamentary implications, was his disclosure that £70 million is to be earmarked in the next financial year for spending on the takeover of private rented property. This is the first step towards fulfilling an election pledge spelled out in our London manifesto. But this cash must be approved by Parliament first and there are no illusions about what that is likely to mean. The Government will seek to clamp down and there is sure to be a bitter Commons battle in the autumn on this.

The last official vote of the session was on a three-line Whip at 10 o'clock. The familiar issue: pay and prices. I listened to the closing speeches from Tony Benn, for us, and Sir Geoffrey Howe, for the Government. Tony is always eloquent and lively, whatever emotions he may fan. Howe is eloquent and soporific. He creates the impression that he has been put up to speak in a deliberate bid to lower the Parliamentary temperature.

We herded into the lobbies for the last time until next October. A good many Members will skip tomorrow and Wednesday when there is little meaningful business expected before the House. There was a holiday spirit abroad as we trooped off home.

24th, Tuesday: Over lunch, advertising industry representatives put forward their proposals for running a fourth TV channel – on commercial lines, of course. Their plan has already gone to the Government and to the Independent Broadcasting Authority. Yesterday they lunched a group of Tory MPs – one of whom apparently dozed off. Today they had invited Labour MPs with broadcasting interests – about eight of us. They laid on a presentation of their viewpoint and answered queries. I doubt if they expected to win overmuch support from Labour Members. I had to leave halfway through the exchanges – after expressing my reservations – to get back to the House for Question Time.

I had an oral question due for reply from Mrs Margaret Thatcher, the Secretary of State for Education, on those computer training schools. It was No. 29 on the Order Paper and might well have been reached. It asked her to seek powers to control and supervise these schools and I wanted to follow up with a supplementary accusing her of 'dragging her high heels' for months, along with other Ministers, on this. But time ran out on me and all I collected was the futile written reply 'No, Sir.' All the questions I have tabled on this issue have now received somewhat negative written answers and, on the face of it, I have got nowhere. But you never can tell. The nagging may have had some effect. It has worried the schools and one interested journalist told me the Government is now to have talks with the British Computer Society about certain aspects.

I also had a question down to Heath asking him to define the allocation of duties to Ministers in the Civil Service Department. It was really intended to flush out into the open the job of Geoffrey Johnson Smith, one of the Parliamentary Secretaries, who does little or no Civil Service work but is primarily responsible behind-the-scenes for ensuring that Ministers present Government policy effectively to the public and don't fall over each other in doing so – an attempt to avoid the mistakes made on occasion by the Labour Government in this respect. But Johnson Smith is never available to be questioned in the House on his activities which are not widely recognised. Once again my luck was out as I had Question 10, though I got a written answer which at least had the merit of confirming this Minister's role.

I had a beer in Annie's Bar where only MPs and political journalists are customers and 'strangers' are not allowed. Then I had a meeting of the Party's special group on communications to discuss in some detail the initial draft of a proposed Green Paper which is likely to be published as a discussion document around the end of the year, outlining our thoughts on policy for the media. By the time I left at nine o'clock the House was near deserted.

25th, Wednesday: The Commons adjourned for the summer recess. There was a final brief flare-up when John Davies, the Government's Common Market Minister, disclosed that we must find an extra £33 million for the Community this year. There was no chance of debating this adequately before the recess but the angry reaction from our side indicated that this issue is set to produce one of the first big rows after the House resumes on October 16th.

Mostly though, the Government will be manoeuvring and manipulating to keep a 'low profile'. A General Election in 1974 is virtually certain (there are few takers for this autumn now). Heath will do his best to trot out a few popular bills and try to keep controversy to a minimum. That way he will severely limit the Opposition's chances to exploit Government mistakes and to occupy a fair share of the headlines.

But politics remains very much an art, not a science. It is unpredictable and unpremeditated for much of the time. Ungovernable outside events are sharply reflected in their effect on Government and Parliament alike. Prime Minister, Front Bencher or Backbencher can foresee the most crucial political developments ahead with no more certainty than the tourists who were milling around Parliament Square, rubbernecking the historic Palace of Westminster buildings, as I drove home.

It would be a dull business if it were otherwise.